WRITE
BETTER ESSAYS

IN JUST 20 MINUTES A DAY

WRITE BETTER ESSAYS
IN JUST 20 MINUTES A DAY

2nd Edition

LEARNINGEXPRESS®

NEW YORK

Library of Congress Cataloging-in-Publication Data:
Write better essays in just 20 minutes a day—2nd ed.
  p. cm.
  Rev. ed. of: Write better essays in just 20 minutes a day / Elizabeth Chesla. 1st ed.
© 2000.
  ISBN 1-57685-546-5
  1. English language—Rhetoric—Problems, exercises, etc. 2. Essays—Authorship—
Problems, exercises, etc. 3. Report writing—Problems, exercises, etc. I. Chesla,
Elizabeth L. Write better essays in just 20 minutes a day. II. LearningExpress
(Organization) III. Title: Write better essays in just twenty minutes a day.
PE1471.C47 2006
808.4—dc22

                                                                          2006000438

Printed in the United States of America

9 8 7 6 5 4 3 2 1

Second Edition

For information or to place an order, contact LearningExpress at:
  55 Broadway
  8th Floor
  New York, NY 10006

Or visit us at:
  www.learnatest.com

Contents

INTRODUCTION   1

PRETEST   7

SECTION 1   **Planning the Essay**   17

LESSON 1   Thinking about Audience and Purpose   19

LESSON 2   Understanding the Assigned Topic   25

LESSON 3   Brainstorming Techniques: Freewriting and Listing   31

LESSON 4   More Brainstorming Techniques: The 5 W's and Mapping   37

LESSON 5   Choosing a Topic and Developing a Thesis   43

LESSON 6   Outlining and Organizational Strategies   49

LESSON 7   More Organizational Strategies   57

SECTION 2   **Drafting the Essay**   63

LESSON 8   Thesis Statements and the Drafting Process   65

LESSON 9   Paragraphs and Topic Sentences   71

LESSON 10   Providing Support   77

LESSON 11   Strategies for Convincing   85

CONTENTS

LESSON 12   Introductions   93

LESSON 13   Conclusions   99

SECTION 3   **Revising, Editing, and Proofreading the Essay**   105

LESSON 14   Revising: The Big Picture   107

LESSON 15   Revising Paragraphs   113

LESSON 16   Editing   121

LESSON 17   Proofreading   131

SECTION 4   **Taking an Essay Exam**   141

LESSON 18   Preparing for an Essay Exam   143

LESSON 19   Drafting, Editing, and Proofreading   151

LESSON 20   Sample Essay Exam Questions and Answers   157

POSTTEST   163

ANSWER KEY   173

ADDITIONAL RESOURCES   193

Introduction ▶

You probably can't even count how many essays you've written for your high school classes. There are essays assigned in English and composition classes, history and civics classes, and language classes. Many electives even require essays. If you're a junior or senior, you know that the stakes for essay writing keep getting higher. You'll probably have to write one in class as part of an exam, and/or have a large part of your grade based on an essay. But they're not just worth grades—essays are also a part of high-stakes tests like the ACT, Regents', and SAT; and they're required on college applications.

How can you improve your essay-writing skills, not only to get better grades, but also to score higher on tests and boost your chance for admission to the college you'd like to attend? This book offers a step-by-step plan that can be completed in just a few weeks.

▶ How to Use This Book

There are 20 lessons in this book, each of which should take you about 20 minutes to complete. If you read five chapters a week and complete the practice exercises carefully, you should become a more powerful and effective essay writer in one month.

Although each lesson is designed to be an effective skill builder on its own, it is important that you proceed through the book in order, from Lesson 1 through Lesson 20. The material in Section 2 references and builds on what you'll learn in Section 1, as Sections 3 and 4 reference and build on Sections 1 and 2. Writing is a process—a series of skills, strategies, and approaches that writers use to create effective essays. In reality, this process isn't as linear this book presents. You might prefer to brainstorm first, and then write a thesis statement—and that's fine. However, once you understand the writing process, you can adapt it to your unique working style and to each specific writing situation you encounter.

The first section of the book, *Planning the Essay*, covers the basic prewriting steps that are essential to effective writing. *Drafting the Essay*, Section 2, shows you how to take your ideas and formulate a solid working draft. In the third section, *Revising, Editing, and Proofreading the Essay*, you'll learn how to shape your draft into a clear, effective essay. *Taking an Essay Exam*, the fourth section, provides strategies for writing under the pressure of a ticking clock, whether for an in-class exam or a test such as the ACT or SAT.

Each lesson includes several practice exercises that allow you to work on the skills presented in that lesson. The exercises aren't simply matching or multiple-choice questions. Instead, you'll practice what you've learned by doing your own writing. These practice exercises are central to your success with this book. No matter now many examples you see, you really won't benefit fully from the lessons *unless you complete the exercises*. Remember to keep your practice answers as you work through the book—some lessons will ask you to further develop ideas generated in earlier practice exercises.

To help you stay on track, use the sample answers and explanations for the practice exercises at the back of the book. Check them at the end of each lesson, reading the explanations carefully as you review your response to the exercise. Keep in mind that there is no single correct answer to most exercises. What you'll find instead are *suggested* answers that contain all the elements called for in the exercise.

You'll also find practical skill-building ideas at the end of each lesson—simple thinking or writing tasks you can do to sharpen the skills you learned in that lesson. Some of these exercises ask you to read an essay and examine it for a specific element or detail. You can find essays in many places, such as an English or composition class textbook, or on the Internet. If you have trouble finding appropriate writing, check the list of suggested reading in the Additional Resources section at the end of the book.

To gauge your progress, we'll begin with a writing pretest. You should take the test before you start Lesson 1. Then, after you've finished Lesson 20, take the posttest. The tests are different but comparable, so you'll be able to see just how much your understanding of the writing process and your writing skills have improved.

▶ Different Types of Essays

What makes writing both interesting and challenging is that every writing task is unique. Writing is communication: You are expressing ideas about a *subject* to an *audience* for a *purpose*. Each time you sit down to write, one or more of these three elements will be different, creating a unique writing situation.

Essays are one of many different forms, or genres, of writing. While there are many different kinds of essays, general skills and strategies apply to all of them. This book will teach you those skills and strategies and help you practice them. Specifically, we'll help you apply those skills and strategies to three essay types:

- The college application essay
- Essays for high school and college classes (timed and untimed)
- The standardized, timed essay exam (such as ACT, GED, Regents', SAT)

Section 4 of this book (Lessons 18, 19, and 20) extensively covers the standardized, timed essay exams. Here is more information about how to approach and successfully complete application and class assignment essays.

The College Application Essay

Most colleges and universities require students to submit a written essay with their application. The nearly 300 schools that use the Common Application (www.commonapp.org) present five topics from which you must select and write on one. Other schools use similar types of topics, or even ask you to come up with your own.

No matter the topic, though, the purpose of this essay remains the same: to reveal something personal about you that will give the admissions department a better idea of who you are and why they should accept you. This isn't the time to wow your reader with your insights into current social problems or the poetry of the seventeenth century. Your audience, an admissions officer, want to learn about *you*. A successful college application essay transforms you from a two-dimensional applicant into a dynamic, three-dimensional "real" person. And in most cases, the more real you are to the admissions officer, the more likely it is that he or she will accept you.

Of course, the application essay also gives the reader a sense of how well you can communicate in writing, and that ability is crucial to your academic success. After all, admissions officers are not only looking to see if you're a good fit for the university—they also want to see that you'll be able to handle their curriculum and that you can read and write effectively at the college level.

Here are some Common Application topics and writing requirements found on most other applications:

1. *Evaluate a significant experience, achievement, risk you have taken, or ethical dilemma you have faced, and its impact on you.*
2. *Discuss some issue of personal, local, national, or international concern and its importance to you.*
3. *Indicate a person who has had a significant influence on you and describe that influence.*
4. *Describe a character in fiction, an historical figure, or a creative work (as in art, music, science, etc.) that has had an influence on you.*
5. *A range of academic interests, personal perspectives, and life experiences adds much to the educational mix. Given your personal background, describe an experience that illustrates what you would bring to the diversity in a college community, or an encounter that demonstrated the importance of diversity to you.*
6. *Topic of your choice.*
7. *Submit a writing sample.*

"Topic of your choice" and "submit a writing sample" allow you to recycle something you've written for a class, or even another application (just be sure to change or delete any references to another school).

No matter which topic you select, remember that it is meant simply as a vehicle for revealing something about *you*, not the historical figure, issue of international importance, or person who has influenced you. But being personal can be tricky. Anything and everything in your life or about your personality is not appropriate admissions-essay material. College admissions officers note that the worst essays are depressing and/or paint an unflattering picture of the applicant. Think of it this way: Your job in the essay is to get the reader to like you. Don't hand him or her a reason to reject you by revealing negative information. Your goal is to sound competent and responsible.

Here are a few other specific strategies to help you write a winning college application essay:

- Avoid clichés. The typical admissions officer reads hundreds of essays each winter. You won't stand out, and you'll run the risk of boring him or her, if you write about a subject also chosen by dozens of other students. What's been done too many times before? Here are a few subjects virtually guaranteed to bore your audience: how you've been influenced by a famous person, the death of a grandparent, losing the big game, why you want peace in the Middle East, etc.

- Think local, not global. The small, uniquely personal experience is more revealing than your response to 9/11 or your plan to solve global warming. "Local," or small, also guarantees that your essay will be original. Choose a subject that you alone have found significance in, and you'll have a better chance of writing the kind of essay they're looking for.

- Don't brag or overstate your importance. There is a fine line between appropriately advocating for yourself and your talents, and sounding like a walking ego. In general, don't take credit for anything you shouldn't (did your team really win the championship because of your leadership skills?).

- Avoid offensive topics. You don't know if your essay will be read by a 20-something, a 70-something, Democrat or Republican, male or female, gay or straight, white or black, Christian or Buddhist. Therefore, the risk of offending this unknown reader is great. You should steer clear of touchy subjects, and be careful not to dismiss or critique the other side of your argument while laying out your own.

Essays for High School and College Classes

In almost every high school or college class, you can expect at least part, if not all, of your evaluation for the term to be based on your written work. In a college literature class, for example, 100% of your grade will probably be based on two out-of-class essays, an in-class midterm, and a final essay, which may be a timed exam. In a political science class, your midterm and final exams might include multiple-choice, short answer, and essay questions. Your success in school depends heavily on your ability to write effectively, both in and out of the classroom.

Types of Essay Assignments

Essay assignments in high school and college classes will be as varied as the instructors who teach them. Most assignments, however, will fall into one of two categories:

1. **The Personal Essay**

   In composition classes and in college placement exams, you will often be asked to write an essay based on a personal experience or observation. Here are two examples:

   Alison Lurie wrote, "Long before I am near enough to talk to you in the street or at a party, you announce your personality and opinions to me through what you are wearing. By the time we meet and converse, we have already spoken to each other in an older and more universal language: the language of clothing." Write an essay in which you agree or disagree with this statement. Use evidence from your personal experience, observations, or reading to support your position.

Tips for Success

Here are some strategies for successful high school and college essays:

- Fulfill the assignment. Have a clear thesis that directly responds to the assignment, and develop it as required.
- Provide solid support. Whether you're writing a personal essay or an analysis essay, you need to show readers that your thesis is valid. Support your ideas with specific examples, evidence, and details.
- Be correct. You need to convey your ideas clearly. Make sure your sentences are clear and free of errors in grammar and mechanics.
- Write with style. Most of your essays will be on the formal side, but that doesn't mean they have to be dull and dry. Choose interesting words that state exactly what you mean, including vivid verbs and specific adjectives and adverbs.

Describe a time when you presented yourself as believing in something you really did not believe in. Why did you present yourself that way? What were the consequences, if any, of this misrepresentation? How would you present yourself in a similar situation today? Explain.

2. The Analysis Essay

In most other classes, essay assignments will often ask you to analyze specific texts, ideas, events, or issues. Here are three examples from different disciplines:

From a religious point of view, what is truth? Use examples from two different religions to support your answer.

Analyze a local television news program. What stories and events get coverage? How are these stories and events covered? What values and beliefs about America, about the world, and about television and its viewers do you think the news program's coverage reflects?

What illusions does Renoir's film La Grande Illusion *refer to? Discuss those illusions and how the historic events that led to World War I helped foster them.*

Pretest

Before you begin this book, it's a good idea to find out how much you already know and how much you need to learn about the essay-writing process. This test is designed to help you do that. It consists of two parts. Part 1 contains 20 multiple-choice questions addressing several key components in this book. Part 2 asks you to write your own essay and evaluate it according to the criteria provided.

You can use the space on the pages following Part 2 to record your answers and write your essay. Or, if you prefer, simply circle the answers directly for Part 1. Obviously, if this book doesn't belong to you, use separate sheets of lined paper to write your responses.

Take as much time as you need for Part 1 (although 20 minutes is an average completion time). When you're finished, check your answers against the answer key at the end of this book. Each answer tells you which lesson deals with the concept addressed in that question. Set aside another 30 minutes to complete Part 2.

1. (a) (b)
2. (a) (b) (c) (d)
3. (a) (b) (c) (d) (e)
4. (a) (b)
5. (a) (b) (c) (d)
6. (a) (b) (c) (d)
7. (a) (b) (c) (d)

8. (a) (b) (c) (d)
9. (a) (b) (c) (d)
10. (a) (b) (c) (d)
11. (a) (b) (c) (d)
12. (a) (b) (c) (d)
13. (a) (b) (c) (d)
14. (a) (b) (c) (d)

15. (a) (b) (c) (d)
16. (a) (b)
17. (a) (b) (c) (d) (e)
18. (a) (b)
19. (a) (b) (c) (d) (e)
20. (a) (b) (c) (d) (e)

► Part 1

1. All essays should be about five or six paragraphs long.
  a. true
  b. false

2. The best place in an essay for the thesis statement is generally
  a. the first sentence in an essay.
  b. the last sentence in an essay.
  c. the end of the introduction.
  d. in the third paragraph.

3. A good introduction should do which of the following?
  a. grab the reader's attention
  b. state the thesis
  c. provide the main supporting ideas for the thesis
  d. both **a** and **b**
  e. all of the above

4. Your relationship with your readers has an effect on how you write your essay.
  a. true
  b. false

5. Which of the following best describes the problem with the following paragraph?
  Sullivan studied 25 city playgrounds. He found several serious problems. The playgrounds were dirty. They were also overcrowded. They were also dangerous. Many parks had broken glass everywhere. Many parks also had broken equipment.
  a. lack of variety in sentence structure
  b. grammatical errors
  c. lack of transitions
  d. poor word choice

6. Which organizational strategy does the paragraph in question 5 use?
  a. compare and contrast
  b. chronology
  c. problem → solution
  d. order of importance

7. Read the following essay assignment carefully.

Some say "ignorance is bliss." Others claim that ignorance is a form of slavery and that only knowledge can set you free. With which view do you agree? Explain your answer.

Determine which sentence below best describes the kind of essay you should write.

a. Explain the difference between "ignorance" and "knowledge."

b. Explain which belief you concur with and why.

c. Explain how you think we can improve education.

d. Discuss the evils of slavery.

8. Which of the following organizational patterns applies to all essays?

a. order of importance

b. cause and effect

c. assertion → support

d. problem → solution

9. A *thesis* is best defined as

a. the prompt for an essay.

b. the main idea of an essay.

c. an essay that is at least three pages long.

d. the way a writer introduces an essay.

10. In the following paragraph, the first sentence is best described as which of the following?

More and more Americans are turning to alternative medicine. The ancient art of aromatherapy has gained a tremendous following, particularly on the West Coast. Acupuncture, the traditional Chinese art of "needle therapy," has doubled its number of active practitioners in the past decade. And holistic medicine—treating the whole body instead of just one part—is so popular that some HMOs now even pay for holistic care.

a. a transition sentence

b. a topic sentence

c. a supporting idea

d. a thesis

11. In the paragraph in question 10, the second sentence is best described as which of the following?

a. a transition sentence

b. a topic sentence

c. a supporting idea

d. a thesis

12. Which of the following should a conclusion NOT do?

a. Bring in a new idea.

b. Restate the thesis in fresh words.

c. Provide a sense of closure.

d. Focus on the reader's emotions.

13. Words and phrases like *meanwhile, on the other hand,* and *for example* are known as
    a. passive words.
    b. assertions.
    c. modifiers.
    d. transitions.

14. Which of the following strategies is particularly useful during an essay exam?
    a. brainstorming
    b. freewriting
    c. outlining
    d. journaling

15. Brainstorming typically takes place during which step in the writing process?
    a. planning
    b. drafting
    c. proofreading
    d. revising

16. *Revising* and *proofreading* are interchangeable terms.
    a. true
    b. false

17. Support for a thesis can come in which of the following forms?
    a. specific examples
    b. expert opinion
    c. anecdotes
    d. both **a** and **b**
    e. **a**, **b**, and **c**

18. Never use a one-sentence paragraph.
    a. true
    b. false

19. What is the main problem with the following sentence?
Newman lost the election because of the fact that the opponent whom he ran against had a lot more money for ads.
    a. It's a run-on sentence.
    b. It's not properly punctuated.
    c. It's unnecessarily wordy.
    d. It lacks parallel structure.
    e. There is no problem with this sentence.

20. Which of the following strategies will make an essay more convincing?
   a. avoiding run-on sentences
   b. acknowledging counterarguments
   c. providing specific examples and details
   d. both **b** and **c**
   e. both **a** and **c**

▶ Part 2

Set a timer for 30 minutes. When you're ready to begin, carefully read the following essay assignment. Use the space provided to write your essay. Stop writing when 20 minutes have elapsed, even if you haven't completed your essay. When you're finished, look at the scoring chart in the answer key to estimate your essay's score.

Essay Assignment

Many people have been profoundly affected by great works of art. Describe a work of art—a book, a movie, a photograph, a drawing, a painting, a song, or a musical composition—that had a powerful impact on your life. What work of art was it? How did it affect you? Why?

1 ▶ Planning the Essay

WHILE CREATIVITY AND inspiration can play an important role in good essay writing, planning, drafting, and revision are critical. Whether you have to write an essay in class, during a test, or at home, getting down to the business of writing means focusing on these three things. In this section, you'll learn planning strategies that will not only improve the effectiveness and quality of your writing, but will also help eliminate many of the frustrations writers face. In addition, they'll benefit your reader by showing him or her how the various points you make in your essay work together and how they support your thesis.

When you begin your essay with planning, you will have guidance and direction through the writing process, especially if you are in a timed situation. Planning lets you see how your many developing ideas fit within a framework, and clearly maps out any type of essay you are required to write.

▶ Thinking about Audience and Purpose

LESSON SUMMARY

The first step toward effective essay writing is to know why and for whom you're writing. This lesson explains how to understand your audience and purpose and how these two factors affect your writing.

magine you've just had an amazing experience: You were able to save someone's life by performing CPR. You want to share the experience with three people: your father, your best friend, and the admissions officer at your first-choice college. How will you describe what happened? Will that description be the same for each person? Probably not. Although the subject remains a constant, each person is a different *audience*, requiring different word choices, levels of formality, and tone.

Because you are sharing the experience with these three people for different reasons, the *purpose* of your description changes, too. You might tell your father to let him know that his advice about taking a CPR course was invaluable. To your friend, you might stress the emotions the experience evoked. In your college application essay, you place an emphasis on the experience's revelation of your competent and responsible nature.

Audience and purpose not only determine *how* you write; they shape your content, or *what* you write as well. Therefore, the first step to writing better essays is to understand who you are writing for and why you are writing.

▶ Understanding Your Audience

Imagine that you've been asked to write about your life-saving experience for the local hospital newsletter. You expect your audience to be adults, so you plan and draft your article in anticipation of that audience. But when you submit it, you find that the hospital plans to use your article in a supplement for elementary school students. Can they print it as written? Not if they want their readers to understand what you've written.

Understanding your audience is a critical component of effective writing. Before you begin any type of essay, you must find out:

1. Who will read your essay and why are they reading it?
2. What do they know about your subject?
3. What is your relationship with the reader?

Pinpointing Your Audience

If you're writing for a teacher, you know his or her name and face, as well as the expectations he or she has for your writing. But determining your audience doesn't always mean knowing exactly who will be reading, grading, or scoring your essay. In fact, often you'll need to write for someone, or a number of people, you'll never meet. For example, if you are taking the ACT or SAT, you know that two people will read your essay and score it. You also know the criteria for each score. You don't know the readers' names, or where they're from, but you know enough about what they're looking for to understand how to write to them. Knowing your audience in this case means knowing what they're looking for.

In other words, your readers will pick up your writing in order to give it a grade or score. You need to know their expectations in order to fulfill them. What does your English teacher consider an A essay? How does a college admissions officer judge an essay? For the SAT and ACT, what does the scoring rubric look like? What are the differences between an essay that gets a 6, and one that gets a 2? Here are some general guidelines:

WHO THEY ARE	WHAT THEY'RE LOOKING FOR
Admissions officer	an engaging essay that reveals your personality, goals, and values; evidence that you can organize your thoughts and communicate effectively
SAT and ACT scorers	a polished rough draft that responds to the topic, develops a point of view, and supports that point of view with examples and evidence
AP Exam evaluators	a clear and cohesive essay that demonstrates mastery of the subject matter
High school teachers	a combination of the following: mastery of the material (do you understand the book, concept, issue?); a clear and original thesis; mastery of the essay form (clear thesis, strong support, logical organization); mastery of standard written English

Here's an example. Imagine that you have been asked to write about a poem. Clearly, you could not write the same essay for a college application and an English Literature AP exam. You have two different sets of actual readers who want two very different things from you.

Admissions officers, for example, would prefer a very personal response to the poem, one that reveals something about who you are and what is important to you. They might want to know if the poem helps you better understand something about yourself and your values. They might want to know how you understand the poem. What does it mean to you? How does it make you feel? What do you get out of it? How can you relate it to your life?

The Audience's Relationship to the Subject

In addition, it's essential to consider the relationship of your audience to your subject. What are they likely to know about your topic? How interested will they be in what you have to say? How likely are they to agree or disagree with your ideas?

What Your Readers Know about the Subject

One of the biggest mistakes writers make is to assume that their readers know what they're talking about. Just because you know your subject intimately doesn't mean your readers do. You need to carefully consider how much your readers may know about your subject. For example, you've decided to write about your interest in robotics for your college application essay. If you use terms like "range weighted Hough Transform" and "sensor fusion algorithm," chances are your readers won't know what you're talking about. You'll either have to explain your terms or replace the technical jargon with words the average reader can understand.

Similarly, say you decide to write about your favorite novel. Should you assume your readers have read the novel? If they have, should you assume that they read it recently enough to remember its characters, plot, and themes? Unless you know for sure, or unless your assignment specifically mentions an assumption ("assume your readers have read *The Great Gatsby* carefully"), you must provide sufficient background information for your readers. You'll need to briefly summarize the plot and provide context for the specific scenes and issues you'd like to discuss.

How Your Readers Feel about the Subject

Another important consideration is how your readers might feel about the subject. Will they be interested in it? If not, what can you do to arouse their interest? If you've taken a position on an issue, how likely is it that your readers will share your opinion? If they're likely to disagree, how can you help them accept, or at least understand, your position? (You'll learn more about this issue in Lesson 11.)

Your Relationship to the Reader

Finally, there's one more question to ask about your audience: What is your relationship to him or her? This relationship helps determine the style, tone, and format of your essay.

Though the writing situations discussed in this book are different, your relationship to the actual reader is quite similar in each case: that of evaluatee to evaluator. The primary reason your actual readers—college admission officers, SAT and ACT scorers, AP essay exam readers, and teachers—are reading your essay is not for their reading pleasure. Instead, they are reading to evaluate.

How does this relationship affect your writing? For most situations, it is in your best interest to be formal (but not stuffy), respectful (but not overly gracious), and courteous (but not ceremonious). You must also follow the provided guidelines or expectations. For example, if your instructor wants your essay typed in a 12-point font, double-spaced, with one-inch margins, and one staple in the top left-hand corner, that's exactly what you should hand in.

▶ Practice 1

1. Briefly explain how to write for an audience that will remain unknown to you personally.

_____

_____

_____

2. *A Martian has just landed in your backyard. He asks where he's landed. You answer, "America." "What kind of place is America?" he replies.*

   a. Who is your audience for this writing assignment?

   _____

   b. Given your audience, how should you approach your topic, and why?

   _____

   _____

   _____

▶ Knowing Your Purpose

Whether you're writing a college application essay or an essay for your political science class, one of your goals is to receive a positive evaluation for your essay. But for that to happen, the essay itself must have a clear purpose.

As important as knowing whom you're writing for is knowing why you're writing. What is the goal of your essay? What are you hoping to convey through your writing? If your essay effectively achieves its purpose, you're more likely to achieve your goal of a high grade or score.

To help you clarify your purpose, you can try a simple fill-in-the-blank:

My goal in this essay is to _____ .

Try to find a verb, or verbs, that best describe what you want your essay to do. For example:

My goal in the essay is to: *demonstrate* that I am a resourceful person.

explain why I took a year off after high school and *show* how that year prepared me for college.

prove that Victor Frankenstein, rather than his creature, is the monster.

Here are some other verbs that can help define purpose:

compare	*describe*	*propose*
contrast	*encourage*	*review*
convince	*explore*	*show*
defend	*inform*	*summarize*

Notice how the verb specifies purpose in the following example:

Herman Melville wrote, "He who never made a mistake never made a discovery." In an essay, describe how a mistake you made led to an important discovery.

My goal is to show how my mistake taught me an important lesson: If you don't follow directions, someone can get hurt.

By clarifying your audience and purpose, you can help ensure that your essay does what it's supposed to, and that its content, structure, and style will be right for its audience. Knowing what you want to say, to whom, and why, should always be the first step in the writing process.

▶ Practice 2

For this assignment, how would you describe your purpose?

Read Langston Hughes's essay "Salvation." In an essay, discuss the central conflict that Hughes describes. How does Hughes resolve that conflict?

_____

_____

▶ In Short

Effective writing begins with a clear understanding of audience and purpose. Know your audience: who will read your essay, why they will read it, and what they already know about your subject. Consider your relationship to your readers, and be sure to carefully consider your purpose. Why are you writing? What do you hope to achieve in your essay?

Skill Building until Next Time

Because a clear sense of audience and purpose is essential to good writing, you should be able to determine the intended audience and purpose of a given text. Select an article from a magazine or newspaper, and read it carefully. Who is the primary audience? What was the writer trying to achieve?

2 ▶ Understanding the Assigned Topic

LESSON SUMMARY

This lesson explains how to break down an assignment to understand exactly what is required.

Whether you like the freedom of choosing your own topic or prefer to have the topic chosen for you, one thing is certain: If you are writing an essay for a college application, the SAT or ACT, an AP Exam, or a high school course, you must fulfill the assignment. If the assignment asks you to write about a particular issue—year-round school, for example—you can't expect to succeed if you write about the need for campaign finance reform. On the SAT, failure to address the topic is grounds for a score of zero— no matter how well you wrote your essay.

Even the most open-ended essay assignments have guidelines that must be followed. There may be a specific issue to address, an approach to take, or a length requirement to fulfill. When the assignment isn't open ended, there are even more constraints. But that's not necessarily a bad thing. Assignments give you a framework within which to work. That framework can not only guide you through the writing process, but can also eliminate the time you would otherwise spend deciding on a suitable topic.

► Fulfilling the Assignment

The essay assignments found on college applications, AP Exams, and the SAT and ACT are the product of considerable study and research. They are designed to elicit essays that fulfill a specific need. Colleges need to know more about you in order to make admissions decisions, so they ask you to write about personal issues. The ACT and SAT writing tests are designed to give colleges and universities a better idea of your writing aptitude. Even your high school teacher, when he or she hands out an essay assignment, is looking for something specific.

You may think that writing about something other than what's assigned portrays you as an independent thinker, someone who can come up with ideas and doesn't need to be told what to do. But that's not the message you'd be sending. If you're doing your own thing and avoiding the topic, you're telling your readers that you don't care about what they want, you don't understand the topic, or you don't know enough about the assigned material to write about it.

Fulfilling the assignment, on the other hand, sends a positive message to readers. It tells them that:

1. You know how to follow directions.
2. You can handle the subject matter.
3. You can meet the challenge presented to you.

Additionally, in timed situations, fulfilling the assignment shows that:

4. You can organize your thoughts about a specific topic while under pressure.

Understanding the Assignment

In order to fulfill the assignment, you must understand exactly what the assignment is asking you to do. While this sounds simple, consider that many essay assignments aren't obvious. What does it mean, for example, to "discuss" an experience? How are you supposed to "analyze" an issue?

Breaking Down the Assignment

To comprehend an assignment, you need to understand the following:

- What you are to respond to (the topic)
- How you are to respond to it

In some cases, there may be more than one topic and more than one way you are supposed to respond. To find out the expectations, break down the assignment. First, underline the words that describe the topic. Then, circle all of the words that tell you how to respond. These "direction words" include *analyze, describe, discuss, explain, evaluate, identify, illustrate,* and *argue.*

For example, here is a writing assignment from an AP Biology exam:

Describe the chemical nature of genes. Discuss the replicative process of DNA in eukaryotic organisms. Be sure to include the various types of gene mutations that can occur during replication.

By breaking down the assignment, you can identify three subjects, each with its own direction word. The subjects are underlined and the direction words are circled:

Describe the chemical nature of genes. Discuss the replicative process of DNA in eukaryotic organisms. Be sure to include the various types of gene mutations that can occur during replication.

To help make the assignment even more manageable, break down the two parts (topic and direction words) into a simple chart:

SUBJECT	DIRECTIONS
1. the chemical nature of genes	describe
2. the replicative process of DNA in eukaryotic organisms	discuss
3. the various types of gene mutations that can occur during replication	include

To completely fulfill the assignment, you must cover all three of these subjects in the manner in which the assignment dictates.

When the Assignment Is a Question

In some assignments, you are given questions instead of direction words. Here's an example:

What were the issues, successes, and failures of the Civil Rights movement from the 1960s through the 1970s?

Notice that there are no direction words. For this type of essay prompt, you will need to determine the word or words yourself. Reread the question, paying careful attention to each word. Notice it begins with *What were*. This is a good clue that you should *identify* the issues, successes, and failures.

Translating questions into directions can be tricky, but it's a critical step in understanding the prompt. You need to determine exactly how you're supposed to respond to the subject. The following chart lists common question words and corresponding direction words.

QUESTION WORDS	WHAT THEY USUALLY MEAN
What is/are . . .	define or identify
What caused . . .	identify or explain
How are/does . . .	explain or evaluate
How is *X* like . . .	compare
How is *X* different . . .	contrast
In what way . . .	illustrate
Do you agree?	argue
Why is/does . . .	explain
What do you think of *X*?	evaluate

▶ Practice 1

Read the essay topics carefully. Use the subject and directions columns in the tables provided to break them down into parts. (Note: You may not need to fill each table.)

1. *Describe the change in citizens' attitudes toward the federal government in the last decade. Explain what you believe to be the causes of this change. Finally, assess the impact of this attitude on the power of the government.*

SUBJECT	DIRECTIONS

2. *In Alice Walker's novel* The Color Purple, *does Celie have control over her destiny? Explain your answer.*

SUBJECT	DIRECTIONS

3. *Describe in detail the current definition of a planet. How does it differ from the definitions of stars and asteroids? If size becomes a defining characteristic of a planet, how will that change the solar system as we know it today?*

SUBJECT	DIRECTIONS

Understanding Direction Words

You've broken down the assignment and isolated the direction words. But what do those direction words really mean? In the following table, you'll find the most common essay direction words and their explanations.

TERM	MEANING
Analyze	Divide the issue into its main parts and discuss each part. Consider how the parts interact and how they work together to form the whole.
Argue	Express your opinion about the subject, and support it with evidence, examples, and details.
Assess	See *evaluate*.
Classify	Organize the subject into groups and explain why the groupings make sense.
Compare	Point out similarities.
Contrast	Point out differences.
Define	Give the meaning of the subject.
Describe	Show readers what the subject is like; give an account of the subject.
Discuss	Point out the main issues or characteristics of the subject and elaborate.
Evaluate	Make a judgment about the effectiveness and success of the subject. What is good and bad about it? Why? Describe your criteria for your judgment.
Explain	Make your position, issue, process, etc. clear by analyzing, defining, comparing, contrasting, or illustrating.
Identify	Name and describe.
Illustrate	Provide examples of the subject.
Indicate	Explain what you think the subject means and how you came to that interpretation (what makes you conclude that it means *X*).
Relate	Point out and discuss any connections.
Summarize	Describe the main ideas or points.

Here are a couple of examples:

Compare and contrast prohibition and the current anti-tobacco movement.

This assignment gives you two direction words: *compare* and *contrast*. Therefore, you should locate and discuss the similarities and differences between the two subjects (prohibition and the anti-tobacco movement).

Rousseau offers judgments about the relative goodness and badness of life as a savage and of life in society. Assess the validity of these judgments. What arguments does he provide to support them? Are they sound arguments?

The explicit direction word in this assignment is *assess*. The implied direction word for the first question "What arguments does he provide to support them?" is *identify*. The implied direction word for the second question "Are they sound arguments?" is *evaluate*. For this assignment, you are expected to:

1. Assess the validity and soundness of Rousseau's judgments.
2. Identify the arguments he uses to support his judgments.
3. Evaluate the strengths and/or weaknesses of his argument.

▶ Practice 2

Reread the essay topics from Practice 1. Given the direction words, briefly summarize how you would approach each essay. Do not use the specific direction words in your answers.

1. _____

_____

_____

2. _____

_____

_____

3. _____

_____

_____

▶ In Short

For every writing situation you encounter, you must fulfill the requirements of the assignment. Break down the assignment into its parts. Identify the subjects you must cover and the direction words that tell you how to address those subjects. Then you can proceed by writing an essay that meets your evaluator's expectations.

Skill Building until Next Time

When you sit down to write an essay, you probably won't have a copy of the direction word chart from page 29. To familiarize yourself with the meanings of the words, write an assignment using each one.

3 ▶

Brainstorming Techniques: Freewriting and Listing

LESSON SUMMARY

Even the most experienced writers sometimes have trouble coming up with ideas. This lesson teaches you two important techniques for generating ideas.

Many students procrastinate when faced with essay assignments for the same reason—they don't know what to write about. This is especially true when students are free to select the topic. Instead of feeling liberated, they find themselves wishing for specific direction. Nowhere is this more critical than in a timed essay exam, when you have to choose a topic quickly in order to complete the exam within 20 to 30 minutes. Fortunately, a few simple strategies can help you generate ideas for any essay assignment.

▶ Brainstorming Ideas

How do you generate ideas? Some writers stare at a blank page waiting for inspiration, while others dive into a draft hoping ideas will come as they write. Both of these techniques take time and often result in disappointment. There are more productive ways to come up with material for your essay—both in terms of time spent and in the quality of that material. Whether you are assigned a topic, must come up with one on your own, or are writing under a time constraint, taking the time to focus and shape your thoughts will result in a better final product.

The most effective technique for focusing and shaping your thoughts is **brainstorming**—allowing yourself some time to make connections with your subject, noting everything and anything that comes to mind. In this lesson and the next, you'll learn four specific strategies for brainstorming. They may be used both to generate new ideas and to clarify those you already have. Brainstorming can also be used effectively when you are faced with a number of possible essay topics and must determine which is the best vehicle to express your unique thoughts and experiences. Some are better suited to a longer writing process, such as the college admissions essay, while others may be adapted for when you have a shorter period to complete an essay, as with the SAT.

▶ Freewriting

Freewriting is probably the best-known prewriting technique. It works well when you have some thoughts on a topic, but can't envision them as an essay. Freewriting also functions as a developmental tool, nurturing isolated ideas into an essay-worthy one. People who use this technique often surprise themselves with what comes out on paper. It is common to discover a thought or point you didn't realize you had.

Specifically, **freewriting** means spending a predetermined period of time writing nonstop, focusing on a specific topic. In fact, freewriting should be called "flow writing," because the most important aspect to this prewriting technique is the flow, or momentum, that comes when you stay with it. It works best when you write in full sentences, but phrases are also effective. The key is to keep writing, without regard for grammar, spelling, or worthiness of ideas. Your speed will help keep you from editing or discarding any ideas.

Freewriting Example

A student received the following essay assignment:

Adrienne Rich wrote: "Lying is done with words and also with silence." Do you agree? Use your personal experience and/or your observations to support your answer.

Keys to Successful Freewriting

- Resist the temptation to look back at what you have written during the process.
- If you can't stay on topic, keep writing anything to maintain the flow.
- Don't censor yourself; no one will see your freewriting, so commit every thought to paper.
- Follow your ideas wherever they lead you.
- When finished, read your freewriting with a highlighter, noting the most interesting and strongest ideas.
- Try the process again after you've focused your topic; more ideas may be generated.

Here is the result of a short freewriting session:

Do I agree? I think so. Is it a lie if you don't say something when you know something? Not technically, but it has the same effect, doesn't it? I remember when I saw Jay with someone else but I didn't tell Karen. She never came out and asked me if Jay was cheating on her, but I knew. But that's not really a lie is it so what do you call it? But there are more important cases where not telling the truth can be deadly. Like if you know someone is planning to commit a crime, and you don't tell anyone. Didn't someone go to jail for not telling the police she knew about the Oklahoma City bombing before it happened? But that's not a lie, it's just not telling, so not telling is not the same as lying. But it can have equally terrible consequences. I guess the point is that you know a truth but you don't reveal it. So they're not the same but they do the same thing. People can get hurt. Unless you believe what you don't know won't hurt you. But that probably falls into the same category as a white lie. It's the other lies and other silences that are the problem.

During her freewriting session, this student came up with a couple of examples and, through them, found a tentative thesis for her essay. She also brought up some issues that will be central to her argument, including the definition of a lie and whether people have a moral obligation to speak up when they have certain kinds of knowledge. You can also see that the student has several run-on sentences, some repetition, and a very informal style. That is part of the freewriting technique.

► Practice 1

Using a separate sheet of paper or your computer, spend five minutes freewriting on the following essay assignment. Remember, there is no wrong answer for this exercise as long as you address the topic. Keep your pen or your typing fingers moving, don't stop, and don't edit or judge. Just set the timer for five minutes, and write.

In his essay "Urban Strategy," William Rhoden describes a time that he put himself at risk to do what he thought was right. Describe a time when you, like Rhoden, put yourself at risk (physically, socially, emotionally, academically) to do what you thought was right. Was it worth the risk? Why or why not?

► Listing

Listing is similar to freewriting in that it is a timed, flowing exercise meant to elicit many thoughts and ideas on a given topic. However, instead of putting whole sentences or phrases on paper, this prewriting technique involves creating a list. It might contain various individual thoughts, ideas that make sense in a particular order, and/or ideas linked together by association with previous ideas.

Listing is a great brainstorming strategy for collaborative writing projects, which work best when they begin with the entire group collecting ideas. In addition, unlike freewriting, listing works well in a timed writing situation. Even within the 25 minutes allotted for the SAT essay, spend a few minutes first listing your ideas before beginning to write.

- If you are not already being timed, set a timer for at least 15 minutes (the more time you spend, the more and better ideas you will probably come up with).
- Write every word or phrase that comes to mind about your topic. If you have not selected a topic, write an answer to the question(s), "What do I have to say to my audience?" or "What do I want my audience to know about me?"
- As with freewriting, do not edit or censor any ideas, and ignore the rules of spelling, grammar, and punctuation.
- When you are finished, look over the list carefully. Cross out useless information, and organize what is left. Categorize similar items.

In this example, a student used listing to generate ideas for his college application essay.

In your opinion, what is the greatest challenge your generation will face? What ideas do you have for dealing with this issue?

- Being overwhelmed by technology
- Staying in physically touch when everything becomes virtual
- How will we know what's real?
- If people live longer, what about the generation gap?
- Find better ways to take care of parents, and grandparents
- Being overwhelmed by information
- What about the people who don't have access to technology—social inequality
- The environment
- Slow consumption of our resources
- Recycle more
- Come up with alternative fuel sources
- World government?
- Disease—new viruses—bird flu?
- What about our new power for destruction, biowarfare?

▶ Practice 2

Take three to five minutes to brainstorm a list of ideas for the following assignment:

Many forces contribute to our sense of self. What is a strong determining factor for your sense of identity?

_____

_____

_____

_____

_____

_____

_____

▶ In Short

Two effective ways to generate ideas are the freewriting and listing brainstorming techniques. Simply write non-stop about your assignment for a set period of time, either going across the page in sentences (freewriting) or down the page in a list (listing). Don't judge your ideas, and don't edit. The more freely you write, the easier it will be to tap into your creativity—and the more ideas you'll come up with.

Skill Building until Next Time

Use the freewriting and listing techniques for any kind of writing or thinking tasks this week. For example, if you have to buy a gift for a friend, brainstorm a list of ideas. Or, if you have to make an important decision, freewrite about the pros and cons for five minutes.

LESSON

4 ▶ Brainstorming Techniques: The 5 W's and Mapping

LESSON SUMMARY

This lesson describes two more techniques for generating ideas for your essays: asking reporters' questions and mapping.

People learn and process information in many different ways. Some of us learn best by seeing, others by hearing, and still others by doing. Some of us prefer a defined structure or framework, while others think best when there are no constraints. For those who like structure, the **5 W's** (*who, what, where, when, why*) offer an easy framework for generating ideas. For visual learners and thinkers, graphic organization tools like mapping work best.

▶ Asking Questions

Asking "who, what, where, when, and why" is a formula that journalists, detectives, and researchers use to get a complete story. This technique is particularly useful when you're choosing an essay topic and when focusing a topic once you've made a selection. There are two sets of questions for taking stock, one suited for an impersonal or research-type essay, and the other geared toward a personal essay. Unlike some of the other brainstorming techniques, you should ask questions deliberately, with great thought given to each question. Do not rush or include every idea that comes to mind. Even if you are being timed, take a moment to give the best answer you can for each question. The better focused your answers, the more information you will have to use in your essay.

If you are writing a research paper or other type of nonpersonal writing, and your topic is already selected or assigned, concentrate on the standard W's: *who, what, where, when,* and *why.* These questions will help you quickly develop a great deal of information about your subject. Not every question will apply to every essay, and the prompts that follow each *W* are meant to be taken as suggestions. Be flexible, and use the format as it best fits your topic.

1. **Who:** Who is involved? At what level? Who is affected?
2. **What:** What is your topic? What is its significance? What is at stake? What are the issues?
3. **Where:** Where does your subject occur? Where is its source?
4. **When:** When does your topic occur? When did it begin/end? When must action be taken to deal with it?
5. **Why:** Why is your subject of interest? Why did it develop as it did? Why should others be interested in your topic?

Admissions essays and some exit essays are intended to be personal, so you must focus on yourself. Take time answering personal questions such as the following. This process involves a different set of W's, meant to elicit key information about you and about the topic if it has been chosen.

1. **Where** have you been (chronological history)?
2. **What** have you accomplished or achieved?
3. **What** do you do with your time when not in school?
4. **What** are you good at? Passionate about?
5. **Who** are/were your major influences?

Here's how the 5 W's might work for the following assignment:

Television is a very powerful medium. What do you think is the ideal place of television in our lives, and why? Explain. How close is the reality to that ideal?

Who watches TV?

What kinds of shows are people watching?

What happens to kids who watch too much TV? (affects schoolwork, relationships with others?)

What about people who have no TVs? Are they more informed? Less informed?

What do people expect from TV? Relaxation? Information? Entertainment?

Where do people place TVs in their homes? Kids' rooms? (effect on family relationships, socialization?)
  Bedroom? (effect on sleeping/relaxation?) Kitchen? (effect on conversation during meals?)

What effect does TV have on our lives? Hurts us? Helps us?

What if we got rid of TV?

When was TV invented?

Why do people watch TV?

Notice the number of questions and the amount of possible essay material this student was able to generate. Some of the questions are more relevant to the assignment than others ("when was TV invented" probably won't be relevant, for example). But clearly, this student has many ideas to work with. In the next lesson, you'll learn how to use a brainstorming session like this to develop a thesis and organize your essay ideas.

▶ Practice 1

Use the 5 W's technique to generate ideas for the following assignment.

School uniforms for public school students is among the most controversial proposals for education reform in America. Where do you stand on this issue? Defend your position.

_____

_____

_____

_____

_____

_____

▶ Mapping

Mapping is a graphic (visual) organizer that allows you to investigate the relationships between many diverse ideas. It's a simple process best used for exploring simple topics. To make a map, draw a circle and add spokes radiating from it. Put your central idea or subject in the middle, and add subtopics or related ideas around it in any order. Or, draw a box with your subject written in it and continue adding boxes, connected to each other by arrows, showing the development of your idea. As with other brainstorming techniques, don't judge yourself during this process. Write down any and every thought you have on your subject.

Example of a Concept Map

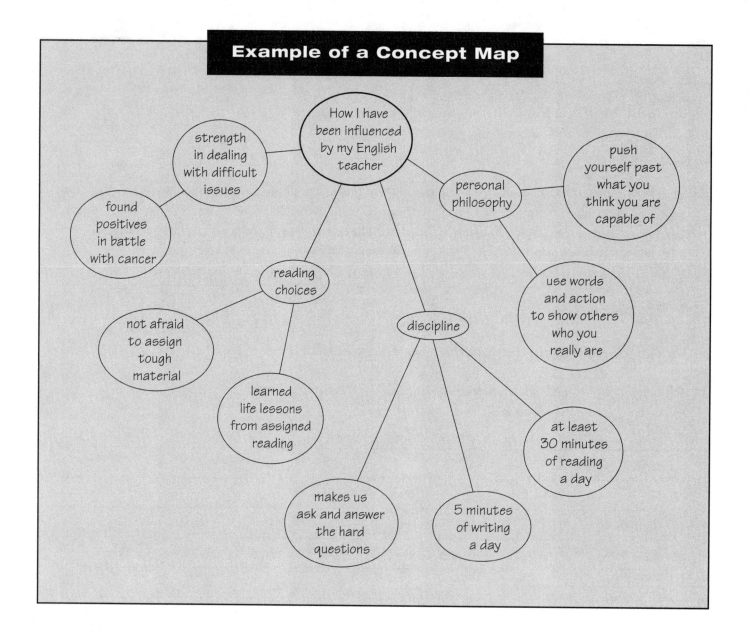

This student came up with four main branches of ideas—discipline, reading choices, personal philosophy, and strength in dealing with difficult issues. The map shows how one idea led to another and how ideas are related to one another. That's an advantage of this technique: You can see immediately where your ideas lie. Clearly, this student has much to say about discipline as it related to his teacher's influence on him.

For the next assignment, notice how the resulting map differs from the previous example.

Discuss how sports influence popular culture.

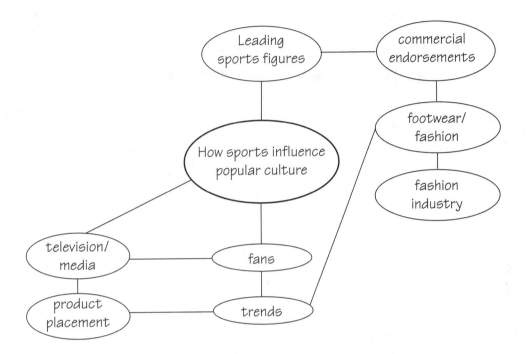

▶ Practice 2

Use the mapping technique to brainstorm ideas for your answer to this college application essay assignment. Write your answer on a separate sheet of paper or type it on your computer.

Write an essay that conveys to the reader a sense of who you are.

A Note about Outlining

Outlining is another important essay-planning tool, but it is not a brainstorming technique. **Outlining** is an organizational technique that helps in planning an essay after ideas have been generated through brainstorming. You'll learn more about outlining in Lesson 6.

▶ In Short

To generate ideas for an essay, try asking questions using the 5 W's: *who, what, where, when,* and *why.* Or try a map: Put your topic in the middle of a page and see your ideas develop in relationship to one another.

Skill Building until Next Time

Use the 5 W's and mapping techniques for any kind of writing or thinking task this week. For example, if you need to decide whether to join the drama club or get a part-time job, you can use the 5 W's technique to help you come up with the pros and cons for each choice. Similarly, you could use the mapping technique to see how taking a part-time job would affect your life.

5 ▶ Choosing a Topic and Developing a Thesis

LESSON SUMMARY

This lesson explains how to narrow your topic so that it is sufficiently focused. You'll also learn how to develop a tentative thesis for your essay.

You've done some brainstorming and you've generated many ideas. Now, how do you turn those ideas into an essay?

First, accept that many of those ideas will never go farther than your brainstorming notes. Think of the brainstorming process of as a type of "rehearsal," in which you try on different ideas or approaches. You won't be able to use them all. Instead, you'll choose the very best for your "performance" (your essay). Somewhere in your brainstorming notes is at least one great idea that you can develop into an effective essay.

► Rules of Thumb for Choosing a Topic

The writing process involves making many decisions. You begin by deciding what to write about. To ensure that you make a good choice, follow these four rules. The topic you choose must:

1. be interesting to you and your audience
2. fulfill the writing assignment
3. be sufficiently focused
4. be able to be turned into a question

Capturing Interest

The first rule for choosing a topic is simple: Make certain it holds your interest. If it's not interesting to you, why would it be to your reader? Your lack of enthusiasm will be evident, and your writing is likely to be dull, dry, and uninspired as a result. If you are interested in your topic, you can convey that feeling to your reader, no matter what the subject. Your reader will be drawn in by your lively prose and passionate assertions.

But what if you aren't really interested in any of the ideas you came up with while brainstorming? What if the assignment is about a subject you find dull? The challenge in this situation is to find some approach to the topic that does interest you. For example, your contemporary American politics teacher has asked you to write an essay about a healthcare policy issue—something you've never thought or cared much about. Your first brainstorming session resulted in a number of ideas, but nothing interesting enough to keep you writing for five pages. In that case, it makes sense to brainstorm again, using another method.

Before you begin, make a short list of some of the things that do interest you. Even if they seem totally unrelated to the subject, you may be able to make a connection. For example, one student listed the following five areas of interest:

- music
- driving
- snowboarding
- Tom Clancy novels
- the Internet

She then saw several possible connections with her topic, even before brainstorming again. She could write about healthcare coverage for music therapy, healthcare policy resources on the Internet, or how accident statistics affect healthcare policies.

Finding a Focus

Essay assignments often ask you to write about a very broad subject area. For example, your topic might be to write about the Cold War or about a novel you read in class. You can approach such boundless assignments in many ways.

To write a successful essay, you need to focus your topic. If, for example, you are given the topic of genetic engineering, you must find a specific issue or idea within that broad topic. Otherwise, you will have enough material for a book. You might decide to write about how genetic engineering is used to find cures for diseases, to create "super" crops, or to plan a family with "designer" children.

In other words, you need to focus your material so it can be adequately covered within the confines of the essay. If you try to cover too much, you'll have to briefly mention many subtopics, without delving into the "meat" of your topic. If your topic is too narrow, though, you'll run out of ideas in a page or two, and probably fail to meet the requirements of your assignment.

It may take time to sufficiently focus the topic. Here's how one student narrowed it down:

Assignment:	Write a statement for your generation.
Broad topic:	My generation
Narrowed topic:	My generation's beliefs
Further narrowed topic:	My generation's beliefs about work
Sufficiently narrowed topic:	My generation's beliefs about the balance between work and play

It took three steps, but her "sufficiently narrowed topic" has the right level of focus and can be adequately examined within the essay structure.

Turning Your Topic into a Question

A **thesis** is the main idea of an essay, and is a response to a topic. In the previous example, the student narrowed her topic to "my generation's beliefs about the balance between work and play." To come up with a thesis, she can restate that topic in the form of a question: "What are my generation's beliefs about the balance between work and play?" The answer to that question might be, "My generation believes that life should be made up of equal parts of work and play."

She might never use that sentence in her essay; she could reword it while writing, or after writing, a first draft. Nevertheless, this exercise gives her a point from which she can launch into writing. Here are two more examples of the evolution of a tentative thesis from an assignment, a focused topic, and a question.

Assignment:	Describe how you think the federal income tax system should be reformed and why.
Broad topic:	Reforming federal tax system
Narrowed topic:	Problems with the federal tax system
Further narrowed topic:	Inequalities in the federal tax system
Sufficiently narrowed topic:	How to eliminate inequalities in the federal tax system
Topic turned into a question:	How can we eliminate inequalities in the federal tax system?
Tentative thesis:	Instituting a flat tax will eliminate inequalities.

Assignment:	Write an essay that explores one of the many issues raised in *Frankenstein.*
Broad topic:	An issue in *Frankenstein*
Narrowed topic:	Responsibility
Sufficiently narrowed topic:	Responsibility of the creator to his creation
Topic turned into a question:	What is the responsibility of the creator to his creation?
Tentative thesis:	If the creation is a living being, then the creator is responsible for nurturing and educating his "child."

When Assignments Ask Questions

Essay assignments that pose a question allow you to quickly formulate a thesis. In fact, they are often called "thesis-bearing" assignments for that reason. For example:

Television is a powerful medium. What do you think is the ideal place of television in our lives, and why? Explain. How close is reality to that ideal?

Both questions are thesis bearing. Here is a student's freewriting response.

I think the ideal place of television is that it should be for information and entertainment, but that it shouldn't be watched too much. The reality is far from the ideal because too many people spend too much time watching TV to the point that they don't communicate with each other or do things that they should be doing to be physically and emotionally healthy (examples: exercise or homework).

This answer is a good tentative thesis. It explains how the student feels about the subject, it responds to the assignment, and it is focused.

▶ Practice 1

For the following assignment, identify a broad topic, narrow it, and turn it into a question and tentative thesis.

Assignment:	Identify a factor that you believe figures strongly in a child's personality development. Explain how that factor may influence the child.
Broad topic:	
Narrowed topic:	
Further narrowed topic:	
Sufficiently narrowed topic:	
Topic turned into a question:	
Tentative thesis:	

▶ Practice 2

Return to one of your brainstorming sheets from Lesson 3 or 4. Use the steps outlined in the four rules for choosing a topic, and write a tentative thesis.

_____

_____

_____

_____

_____

▶ In Short

To write an effective essay, you need a topic that interests you and fulfills the assignment. It must be sufficiently focused so the amount of material you will cover can be adequately explored within the confines of an essay. Narrow down your topic until you can turn it into a specific question. The answer to this question should serve as your tentative thesis—the main idea that you will address and develop in your essay.

Skill Building until Next Time

Choose topics and develop tentative thesis statements for the other three brainstorming exercises you completed in Lessons 3 and 4.

6 ▶ Outlining and Organizational Strategies

LESSON SUMMARY

In this lesson, you'll learn about the underlying structure of an essay and how to create an outline. We'll also examine some of the common organizational strategies used by essay writers.

ow that you have a tentative thesis, you may be tempted to jump right in and start drafting. Sometimes, this approach works, especially if you've done a lot of brainstorming, have thought carefully about your assignment, and your writing skills are strong. More often, however, a great essay is the product not only of brainstorming, but of organization as well.

▶ The Assertion → Support Structure

Before discussing common organizational strategies, it's important to consider the underlying structure of essays. Whether an essay is organized by chronology, comparison and contrast, cause and effect, or some other strategy, every essay has the same underlying structure: assertion → support. That is, the essay **asserts** an idea (its thesis) and then **supports** the thesis with specific examples, evidence, and details.

This assertion → support structure is then repeated throughout the essay on many levels. The ideas that provide support for the thesis (major support) are assertions themselves, and therefore need support. The structure then looks something like this:

Main idea (thesis)

  Major supporting idea
    Minor supporting idea
      Support
    Minor supporting idea
      Support
  Major supporting idea
    Minor supporting idea
      Support

The exact underlying structure will vary depending upon the number and type of supporting ideas, but in all its variations, it is the foundation for most essays.

▶ The Benefits of an Outline

Generating an outline before you draft an essay will help you in several ways. First, it will give structure to your ideas. By mapping out the order in which those ideas will flow, you create a roadmap for the drafting process. The roadmap assures that you won't veer off topic, helps prevent writer's block, and speeds up drafting.

  Second, an outline will help you determine where you need more support for your thesis. When you create an outline, you'll be able to see any gaps in the development of your ideas. Strongly supported assertions stand out in contrast to weaker ones.

  Third, an outline will help judge the plausibility of your thesis. If you jump into drafting without organizing first, you may find during the writing process that your thesis doesn't hold up. A good outline can help you revise, modify, and/or strengthen your thesis before you begin writing. Specifically, a good outline will tell you if your thesis is:

- **too broad.** If you have trouble including everything in your outline, you probably have too much to say. Your thesis needs to be more focused.
- **too narrow.** If you can't seem to find enough to say, your thesis might be too focused. You need to broaden it to create a viable essay.
- **unreasonable.** If there isn't sufficient evidence to support your thesis, you should reconsider its viability. You may need to take a different stance.
- **underdeveloped.** If you have many gaps in our outline, you may need to do more thinking or research to find sufficient support.

▶ Kinds of Outlines

If you have to drive somewhere you've never been before, you could just get in the car and start driving, hoping your sense of direction will be enough to land you at your destination. More likely, though, you will consult a map and write down some directions. But how carefully should you plan your trip? Do you want to map out each gas station where you'll need to fill up, and each rest stop where you'll get coffee? Or do you simply need a list of route numbers and turns you'll need to take?

How thoroughly you map out your trip depends on many different factors, such as your familiarity with the terrain and the distance you'll be traveling. The same is true in writing. Do you need a detailed, formal outline that lists every major and minor supporting idea, or just a rough "scratch" outline? Again, the answer depends upon several factors, including how comfortable you are with your thesis, how well you follow a structured outline, and how many ideas you've developed through you brainstorming sessions. It also depends upon the writing situation. During a timed essay exam, you'll only have time to make a list of paragraphs and, very generally, what you'll write about in each one.

Informal Outlines

An **informal**, **rough**, or **scratch outline** is one that lists only the major supporting ideas in the order in which you think you should develop them. Here's an example on an informal outline.

Assignment: Evaluate the proposal to replace the current graded income tax system with a flat tax. Should we institute a flat tax system? Why or why not?

1. Introduction—thesis: A flat tax would be good for the government and for citizens.
2. Problems with current system
3. How flat tax works
4. Benefits of flat tax system
    a. for government
    b. for citizens
5. Conclusion

This outline provides a general structure for a draft. It's not very detailed—it doesn't include the minor supporting ideas or specific examples the essay needs to be fully developed, but it can function well as a roadmap to guide the writer through a first draft.

Formal Outlines

A **formal outline** is much more detailed. It includes specific, supporting details and several levels of support. Here's a part of a formal outline for the same assignment:

I. Describe problems with the current system.
   A. complex
      1. tax rates vary greatly
      2. too many intricate details
   B. unfair
      1. deductions, loopholes, special interests
      2. people with same income can pay different amount of taxes
   C. wasteful
      1. different forms for different people
      2. huge administrative costs
      3. huge compliance costs
      4. advising costs

II. How flat tax works
   A. all citizens pay same rate—17%—for income over a set minimum
   B. all citizens get same personal exemption
   C. no breaks for special interest
   D. no loopholes

III. Benefits
   A. citizens
      1. sense of fairness—all treated equally
      2. poorest pay no taxes
      3. simple to calculate and file
      4. families save more
      5. more faith in government
      6. people will save and invest more
   B. government
      1. streamline IRS
         a. reduce cost
            i. fewer employees
            ii. less paper, printing, etc.
            iii. less auditing costs
      2. healthier economy

▶ Common Organizational Strategies

Essay organization doesn't stop, however, with the underlying assertion ➝ support structure and an outline. A number of effective strategies can organize your information and ideas, comprising a logical, easy-to-understand flow for your essay.

Chronological/Sequential

One way to organize your material is by **chronology**, or **time sequence**. Put ideas in the order in which they happened, should happen, or will happen. This method works best when you are narrating or describing an experience, procedure, or process. Imagine writing about the way a bill is passed in Congress, but the steps needed to complete the process are out of chronological or sequential order. The point or points you are trying to make about that process will get lost in the ensuing confusion.

Here is a sample rough outline using chronology as its organizing principle.

Assignment: Describe a time when you and a family member experienced a deep sense of conflict or when you sharply disagreed about an important issue. What caused the conflict? What was the outcome? Have your feelings about the matter changed or remained the same? Explain.

Tentative thesis: When I decided to become a vegetarian, my parents refused to support me. It was very difficult to stick to my decision—but I'm glad I did.

Rough outline:

1. telling my family
2. their reactions
3. trying to explain my reasons
4. flashback: taking the "virtual tour" of the slaughterhouse on the Web
5. offering to take my family on the tour, but only Wei watching it with me
6. Mom and Dad refusing to cook special meals for me
7. learning to cook for myself
8. Wei accepting my decision and trying some vegetarian meals with me
9. Wei giving up meat too
10. Mom and Dad accepting our decision and supporting us

▶ Practice 1

On a separate sheet of paper or your computer, create an outline using chronology as your organizational principle. Your outline can be rough or formal. Use one of your brainstorms from Lesson 3 or 4, or one of the brainstorms provided as an example to create your outline.

Cause and Effect

Another way to organize ideas is using **cause and effect**. This method works in either direction:

1. cause → effect: what happened (cause) and what happened as a result (effect)
2. effect → cause: what happened (effect) and why it happened (cause)

Like chronology, cause and effect can be the main organizational structure or it can be used to organize a specific part. It can also be used in combination with other organizing principles. For example, if your assignment were to discuss the events that led to World War I, you would probably use cause and effect as well as chronology to organize your ideas.

Here's part of an outline for an essay about the effects of the Industrial Revolution on city life.

Industries moved to cities
   Large influx of working class from rural areas—looking for jobs
   Crowded, unsanitary conditions
   Children in the streets (unsupervised) or working in factories (uneducated)
   Demand for more hospitals, police, sanitation, social services

Spatial

Ideas can also be organized according to **spatial** principles, from top to bottom, side to side, or inside to outside, for example. This organizational method is particularly useful when you are describing an item or a place. You'd use this strategy to describe the structure of an animal or plant, the room where an important even took place, or a place that is important to you.

The key to using spatial organization effectively is to move around the space or object logically. You are using words to relate something that exists physically or visually, and must help your reader understand your ideas. Don't jump around. What follows is a rough outline for an essay using the spatial organizing principle. The student works from the outside of a cell to the inside as she describes its structure:

Structure of an animal cell:
   1. Plasma membrane
      a. isolates cytoplasm
      b. regulates flow of materials between cytoplasm and environment
      c. allows interaction with other cells

Note about Cause and Effect

Whenever you write about cause and effect, keep in mind that most events have more than one cause, and most actions generate more than one effect.

2. Cytoplasm
   a. contains water, salt, enzymes, proteins
   b. also contains organelles like mitochondria
3. Nuclear envelope
   a. protects nucleus
4. Nucleus
   a. contains cell's DNA

▶ Practice 2

On a separate sheet of paper or your computer, create an outline using either the cause and effect or spatial organizing principle. Your outline can be formal or informal. Use one of your brainstorms from Lesson 3 or 4, or one of the brainstorms provided as an example to create your outline.

▶ In Short

Organizing your ideas to create an effective essay is done on a number of different levels. Underlying all essays is the assertion → support structure. For every idea or assertion you make, you need to provide examples, evidence, and details as support. An outline provides a roadmap that not only helps you in the drafting process, but also lets you see where your ideas may need more development or support. Within the outline, ideas can be arranged using a number of strategies. Chronology or time sequence, cause and effect, and spatial arrangements should be chosen and employed based on the type of information you are writing about.

Skill Building until Next Time

In a well-organized essay, the writer's organizing principle should be very clear. Find an essay that appears to be organized by chronology, cause and effect, or spatial principles. Develop an outline from the text so you can see the organizational structure clearly.

More Organizational Strategies

LESSON SUMMARY

This lesson describes four more organizational strategies for essays: analysis/classification, order of importance, comparison and contrast, and problem → solution.

In the previous lesson, you learned ways to organize ideas according to time and space. Now, you'll examine four additional principles of organization:

1. analysis/classification
2. order of importance
3. comparison and contrast
4. problem → solution

▶ Analysis/Classification

Some essays are best organized by arranging ideas, items, or events by their characteristics or functions. The following assignment is broad enough to describe many different strategies.

Plants and animals protect themselves in many different ways. Describe the various strategies organisms have developed for protection.

It makes sense to group similar strategies together and organize your essay by type (classification). A formal outline to address the assignment might look like this:

I. Appearance
   A. camouflage
      1. moths
      2. flounder
      3. walking stick
   B. warning colors
      1. monarch butterfly
      2. coral snake
      3. South American poisonous frog
   C. mimicry
      1. king snake resembling coral snake
      2. swallowtail butterfly larva resembling snake
      3. snowberry fly resembling jumping spider
II. Chemicals
   A. smoke
      1. squid
      2. octopus
   B. smells
      1. skunks
      2. others?
   C. poisons
      1. spiders
      2. snakes
      3. bombardier beetles
III. Armor
   A. spikes, thorns
      1. roses and thistles
      2. sea urchins
      3. porcupines
   B. shells, hard coverings
      1. nuts
      2. beetles
      3. turtles

Notice how the protective strategies are first classified into three categories: appearance, chemicals, and armor. Each of these categories is then further classified for analysis. Appearance, for example, is broken down into three types of protection strategies: camouflage, warning colors, and mimicry.

▶ Order of Importance

One of the most frequently used organizational strategies, **order of importance** is often the main organizing principle of an essay. Even when it's not, it's used in individual sections and paragraphs. It works in both directions, as cause and effect does. You can begin with the most important, and work toward the least, or begin with the least important, and finish with the most.

Most important generally means *most supportive, most convincing,* or *most striking.* For example, the outline you just read lists several protection strategies. While the overall organizing principle is analysis/classification, most sections within that larger structure are also organized by order of importance. Look again at the section on appearance:

I. Appearance
   A. camouflage
       1. moths
       2. flounder
       3. walking stick
   B. warning colors
       1. monarch butterfly
       2. coral snake
       3. South American poisonous frog
   C. mimicry
       1. king snake resembling coral snake
       2. swallowtail butterfly larva resembling snake
       3. snowberry fly resembling jumping spider

"Appearance" is one of the essays' major supporting ideas. The three minor supporting ideas—camouflage, warning colors, and mimicry—are listed in order of importance. *Camouflage* is the most common and least sophisticated of the three, whereas *mimicry* is the most unique and most compelling way that animals use appearance to protect themselves. And for each of these three supporting ideas, three specific examples are provided. Again, they are listed in order of importance, from the least striking example to the most compelling.

Whenever you're building an argument (and in most essays, that's exactly what you're doing), it's most effective to start with the least important idea and move to the most important. A good argument is like a snowball rolling down a hill. It builds momentum and strength as it rolls, one idea building upon another. And because you're working to convince readers that your assertions are valid, it helps to use this structure. In many cases, your least important ideas are probably also the least controversial and easiest to accept. It makes sense to begin with those that your reader will most likely agree with, and build the reader's trust and acceptance as you work toward more difficult concepts.

▶ Practice 1

On a separate sheet of paper or your computer, create an outline using analysis/classification or order of importance as your organizing principle. Your outline can be formal or informal. Use one of your own brainstorms from Lesson 3 or 4, or one of the brainstorms provided as an example.

▶ Comparison and Contrast

Essays that show the similarities and differences between two or more ideas use the comparison and contrast organizational strategy. This strategy depends upon first having comparable ideas or items. For example, you'd have difficulty writing a successful essay if you wanted to compare Frankenstein's creature with Cinderella. Frankenstein's creature and Pinocchio, on the other hand, *are* comparable items—they're both beings that someone else brought to life. Often, comparable items have a number of aspects that may be compared and contrasted. You might compare and contrast the creation of the figures, their creator's reactions after they come to life, and/or their relationships with their creators.

After you've selected the aspects you'll compare and contrast, there are two ways to organize your discussion: the block technique and the point-by-point technique.

The Block Technique

This method organizes ideas by item (*A* and *B*). First, discuss all the aspects of item *A* (ideas 1, 2, and 3). Then, discuss all of the corresponding aspects of item *B*. The result is two "blocks" of text—a section about item *A*, and one about item *B*. For example:

(*A* = Pinocchio; *B* = Frankenstein's creature)

A1—Pinocchio's creation
A2—Geppetto's reaction
A3—Relationship between Pinocchio and Geppetto

B1—The creature's creation
B2—Frankenstein's reaction
B3—Relationship between the creature and Frankenstein

The Point-by-Point Technique

In this method, you organize ideas by aspect (1, 2, 3) rather than by item, so the result is a direct comparison and contrast of each aspect. Because you put each aspect side by side, readers get to see exactly how the two items measure up, element by element. This is a more sophisticated way of organizing a comparison and contrast essay, and it's easier for your reader to follow. Here's a sample outline.

A1—Pinocchio's creation
B1—The creature's creation

A2—Geppetto's reaction
B2—Frankenstein's reaction

A3—Relationship between Pinocchio and Geppetto
B3—Relationship between the creature and Frankenstein

► Problem → Solution

In this organizing principle, you first identify a problem, and then offer a solution. There is no room for flexibility, because it won't make sense to your reader to offer the solution to a problem without first revealing or discussing that problem. Here's the "solution" section of an outline for an essay about the problem of misinformation on the Internet.

III. Solution
    A. Create "reliability index"
        1. ranks sites for level of credibility
        2. run by not-for-profit; perhaps university or consortium of universities
        3. organization would rate websites on scale of trustworthiness (fact-check, etc.)
            a. Priorities
                i. sites offering information about health and healthcare
                ii. sites offering information about raising children (education, emotional, social development)
                iii. sites offering information about finances and investments
    B. Run awareness campaign
        1. public service announcements
        2. lessons in schools
        3. announcements by all Internet providers

► Practice 2

On a separate sheet of paper or your computer, create an outline using comparison and contrast or problem → solution as your organizing principle. Your outline can be formal or informal. Use one of your own brainstorms from Lesson 3 or 4, or one of the brainstorms provided as an example.

▶ In Short

Analysis, order of importance, comparison and contrast, and problem → solution are four more strategies to help organize your ideas. One strategy can serve as an overall organizing principle, while others may help you organize individual paragraphs and sections of your essay.

Skill Building until Next Time

Look for an essay that uses the analysis/classification, comparison and contrast, order of importance, or problem → solution strategy. Work backward from the text to create an outline that delineates the organizing structure.

2 ▶ Drafting the Essay

OW THAT YOU'VE done some planning, you're warmed up and ready to run. The lessons in this section will show you how to draft a successful essay, from introduction to conclusion. You'll learn how to support your ideas with evidence and details, and how to make arguments that are more convincing.

LESSON

8 ▶ Thesis Statements and the Drafting Process

LESSON SUMMARY

In this lesson, you'll learn how to create a rough draft from your brainstorming notes. You'll also find out how to craft a strong thesis statement.

The planning steps in Section 1 have led you to the next stage in the process, writing a rough draft. You broke down the assignment, brainstormed ideas, focused your topic, developed a tentative thesis, and sketched an outline. All of that work has provided a framework that you can now flesh out with sentences and paragraphs that bring your ideas to your audience.

▶ What Is Drafting?

To draft means to create a preliminary version or rough form of a text. *Preliminary* and *rough* are the key words. Like brainstorming, drafting is most effective when you allow yourself to write imperfectly. Unless you're writing a timed essay exam, such as for the SAT or ACT, your essay will take final shape after revising. (And even the graders of those timed essays exams make it clear that they're looking for a "polished rough draft," not a perfect piece of writing.) The point of drafting is to get your ideas on paper within the framework you created in the planning stages, but without the pressure of trying to get it exactly right.

Tips on Overcoming Writer's Block

- **Don't know what to say?** Try one of the brainstorming techniques described in Lessons 3 and 4.
- **Don't know where to begin?** Create an outline. This will help you put your ideas in order and give you a road map to follow.
- **Can't think of the right way to start?** Skip the introduction and instead jump into the body of your essay. Once you know where you're going and what you have to say, come back and create an effective introduction.

Instead of staring at a blank piece of paper, at your outline, and then back at the paper, get writing. It's especially important not to waste time trying to write an eloquent, attention-grabbing introduction. The best introductions are typically written *after* the body of the essay, when your ideas and the manner in which you reveal them are on paper. That's why the lesson on introductions doesn't appear until after the lessons on writing good paragraphs and providing support for your ideas and assertions.

▶ Tips for the Drafting Process

Use the following guidelines to help keep your ideas flowing during the drafting stage:

- **Keep your thesis statement and assignment in front of you at all times.** This will keep you focused on what your essay needs to do.
- **Follow your outline, but be flexible.** Don't feel obligated to stick to your original plan if, as you're writing, you come up with a better order of paragraphs, or a new idea.
- **Save your drafts.** Whether they're on paper or on the computer, keep a copy of every version of your essay. (That means, on the computer, you will need to make a copy of your draft into a new document before revising.) You may find that an idea you thought you weren't going to use will have a place in your essay after all.

▶ Practice 1

Briefly describe your typical writing process. How have you handled drafting in the past? What can you do to make drafting more productive?

_____

_____

_____

_____

_____

▶ Drafting a Thesis Statement

While you don't need to start with an introduction, you should have a thesis statement before you begin drafting. Your **thesis** is the main idea of your essay—it succinctly reveals what you're going to say. In Lesson 5, you learned how to narrow your topic and formulate a tentative thesis. Now, you'll either commit to that thesis, or revise it into a workable thesis statement.

Here are a few more considerations:

1. A good thesis statement makes a strong, clear assertion that conveys your attitude about the subject.

No assertion:	*The School of Rock* is about a substitute teacher.
Mild assertion:	*The School of Rock* is an entertaining film about an influential substitute teacher.
Strong assertion:	*The School of Rock* is about how a substitute teacher uses the transformative power of rock and roll to help his students and himself.

2. A good thesis statement strikes the right balance between too broad and too narrow. It needs to be focused enough to encompass just enough material to cover within the spatial confines of the essay, and narrow enough to include enough material that can be supported by evidence.

Too broad:	Animals have developed many strategies for survival.
Some focus:	Animals have developed many strategies to protect themselves.
Focused:	Many animals have developed physical properties that serve to protect them from predators.
Too narrow:	In "The Open Boat," the repetition of "If I am going to be drowned" conveys Crane's theme of the indifference of nature.
Balanced:	In "The Open Boat," Crane uses several stylistic techniques to convey his theme of the indifference of nature.

3. A thesis statement is not simply an announcement of the subject matter. You need to tell readers what you are going to say about your subject.

Announcement:	This paper will discuss some of the erroneous theories about the causes of the Great Depression.
Thesis statement:	The Great Depression was caused neither by the stock market crash of 1929 nor the Smoot Hawley Tariff Act.

4. A thesis statement is not simply a question or list of questions. You still need to tell your reader what idea you are going to develop in your essay (the answer to one or more of your questions).

Question:	Why did Kafka choose to turn Gregor into a giant beetle?
Thesis statement:	Gregor's transformation into a giant beetle is a powerful symbol representing his industrious nature and his role in his family both before and after his transformation.

5. A thesis statement is not simply a statement of fact. It must be an assertion that conveys your ideas about the subject.

Statement of fact:	There are many important similarities between the Perrault and Grimm versions of *Little Red Riding Hood*.
Thesis statement:	Both the Perrault and Grimm Brothers versions of *Little Red Riding Hood* reveal the authors' negative attitudes toward women.

Where Your Thesis Statement Belongs

While there is no rule that states exactly where you should place your thesis statement, because it helps your reader by identifying your purpose, it should appear within the first or second paragraph of your essay. You want your reader to know before they read too much what idea you will develop. Think of it this way: Imagine someone you don't know calls you on the phone. After she introduces herself, you expect that she'll tell you why she's calling. What does she want? If she doesn't tell you, you could become annoyed, suspicious, and even angry. You deserve the courtesy of an explanation, and so does your reader. That explanation is your thesis statement.

While you should have a good working thesis statement to lead you through your draft, it's important to remember that even that statement is a draft. It's your preliminary version, and as you write, you may find you need to revise it. Be flexible. It makes more sense to revise it based on what you've written (if the writing works) than to revise a decent draft to fit your thesis.

The College Admissions Essay Difference

Admissions officers typically spend about three to four minutes on each application essay. They're not bound by any rule that says they have to read each one from start to finish. The best way to guarantee a full read and a better chance that your essay will help the admissions officer put your application in the "yes" pile is to hook the reader, and only gradually reveal your subject. If you hand your subject, and your treatment of that subject, to him or her in the opening paragraph, you're providing a great reason to stop reading.

▶ Practice 2

Revise and improve the following weak thesis statements.

1. In this essay, I will explain why I want to attend Briarwood College.

_____

_____

2. The death penalty is a controversial issue.

_____

_____

3. This novel had an important impact on my life.

_____

_____

4. What would the consequences of censorship on the Internet be?

_____

_____

▶ In Short

Drafts are rough versions of your essay—a chance to get ideas on paper so you can shape them into an effective essay. To get started, draft a thesis statement that makes a strong assertion about your subject. Be sure it's focused and avoid simply making an announcement, asking a question or stating a fact.

Skill Building until Next Time

Read a couple of essays and look for their thesis statements. How do the authors convey their main idea? Where is the thesis statement located?

9 ▶ Paragraphs and Topic Sentences

LESSON SUMMARY

In this lesson, you'll learn about topic sentences and paragraphing formats. With that knowledge, you'll be able to craft great paragraphs.

Imagine opening a novel and seeing that the entire text is one giant paragraph. How would you feel? You'd probably feel overwhelmed and more than a little annoyed with the author. Why didn't he break the text into paragraphs? How are you going to know when he shifts from idea to idea? How inconsiderate!

Paragraphs are so central to good writing that we tend to take them for granted. Nevertheless, it's worth reviewing their function and recognizing the important benefits they provide.

▶ What Are Paragraphs?

By definition, a **paragraph** is one or more sentences about a single idea. They're also one of a writer's most important tools. They divide the text into manageable pieces of information, and lead the reader by signaling the introduction of new ideas.

Like essays, paragraphs generally have three parts:

1. a **beginning** that introduces the topic of the paragraph and often expresses the main idea of that paragraph in a topic sentence
2. a **body** that develops and supports the main idea
3. a **conclusion** that expresses the main idea, if it was expressed in the introduction; offers concluding thoughts about that topic; and/or offers a transition to the next paragraph

Here's an example of a complete paragraph:

The African country of the Democratic Republic of Congo has had a turbulent past. It was colonized by Belgium in the late nineteenth century and officially declared a Belgian territory by King Leopold in 1895. The country, called the Belgian Congo after 1908, was under Belgian rule for 65 years. Then, in 1960, after several years of unrest, Congo was granted independence from Belgium. The country was unstable for several years. Two presidents were elected and deposed, and there was much arguing over who should run the country and how. Finally, in 1965, a man named Mobutu Sese Seko rose to power. Though the country was remarkably rich in resources such as diamonds, under Sese Seko's rule, the people lived in complete squalor. Still, Sese Seko brought some stability to the region. He ruled for 32 years, until the people finally rebelled in 1997.

The first sentence in the paragraph introduced the topic and expressed its main idea; it is the paragraph's topic sentence. The next seven sentences develop and support that idea. Then, the last two sentences conclude the paragraph well. They remind readers of the main idea (the country's unstable past) and lead them into the next paragraph by introducing the 1997 rebellion that removed Sese Seko from power.

▶ Developing Strong Paragraphs

Paragraphs are the essay in microcosm. Just as an essay is driven by one main idea (its thesis), a good paragraph is also held together by one controlling idea. This idea is usually stated in a topic sentence.

Topic Sentences

Topic sentences are like mini thesis statements. Just as your thesis statement expressed the main idea of your essay, **topic sentences** express the main idea of each paragraph. Like a thesis, the main idea must:

1. make an assertion about the subject. This assertion can be fact or opinion. Here are examples of each:
   Fact: Another strategy plants and animals use to protect themselves is mimicry.
   Opinion: The most interesting strategy plants and animals have developed for protection is mimicry.

2. be general enough to encompass all of the ideas in the paragraph. If it isn't, you're probably trying to cover too much material in the paragraph.

It's logical to begin a paragraph with the topic sentence, but there's no rule compelling you to place it there. There are different ways to lay out an argument within a paragraph, and depending on the one you use, your topic sentence might be better as the last line, rather than the first.

Deductive and Inductive Formats

The two most common ways to organize paragraphs are based on logical reasoning strategies. Does it make more sense, given your subject, to present a general idea first, and then support it with specific supporting evidence and examples? Or would it be better to begin with the evidence and examples, and come to a conclusion that's drawn from it?

Deductive Paragraphs

A **deductive paragraph** follows the former example: It begins with the main argument or claim being made about the subject, and concludes with the supporting evidence and details. Here's an example:

I could tell the test results just by the look on his face. He couldn't bring himself to look at me. The blood had drained from his face and he was pale as china. He tried to smile, but the corners of his mouth refused to cooperate. His shoulders dropped and his whole body seemed to buckle under the weight of the news, as if he'd already given up his fight against the disease.

Notice how the paragraph begins with a topic sentence that expresses the main idea—that his look revealed the test result. The rest of the paragraph gives specific details and his expression and body language "prove" that main idea. This general structure also works well for an entire essay.

Inductive Paragraphs

Inductively organized paragraphs begin with the specifics and lead to a general idea. That's why the topic sentence in this type of paragraph comes last—it expresses the conclusion or argument that's been proven by the build up of evidence. For example:

All day, he emptied cartons of CDs. Disc after disc, he sorted them by category, and then by artist. After loading them on a cart, he wheeled them to the racks, and refilled the store's stock in alphabetical order. He knew no one would easily find the music they were looking for without him doing his job, but that satisfaction did little to relieve his boredom.

This paragraph starts with evidence. Then, in a topic sentence at the end, the writer offers the conclusion she has drawn from that evidence.

Of course, not all paragraphs will fit so neatly into the general → specific or specific → general formats and not all paragraphs will have the topic sentence first or last. But the inductive and deductive formats work for most paragraphs, and form the backbone of paragraphing strategy.

Appropriate Paragraph Lengths

There's no specific rule about how long a paragraph should be, but you can follow some guidelines to make your writing easier to read and understand. Long paragraphs are hard on the eye. If you've written a page or more without a paragraph break, take a careful look at your ideas. Can they be broken up logically into two or more paragraphs? To be reader friendly, a typical typed page should have at least one, but preferably, two to four paragraph breaks.

Very short paragraphs look undeveloped, like incomplete thoughts. They should only be used if you have a sentence (or two) that is important enough to be on its own. A one-sentence paragraph has impact. It stands out visually, and the pauses before and after the sentence give more time for it to sink in and take hold. However, one- or two-sentence paragraphs should be used sparingly—no more than one per page, if that often.

Here's the Congo paragraph again, revised to include a very short paragraph:

The African country of the Democratic Republic of Congo has had a turbulent past. It was colonized by Belgium in the late nineteenth century and officially declared a Belgian territory by King Leopold in 1895. The country, called the Belgian Congo after 1908, was under Belgian rule for 65 years. Then, in 1960, after several years of unrest, Congo was granted independence from Belgium.

But independence came at a price.

For the next five years, the Congo experienced political and social turmoil. Two presidents were elected and deposed, and there was much arguing over who should run the country and how. Finally, in 1965, a man named Mobutu Sese Seko rose to power. Though the country was remarkably rich in resources such as diamonds, under Sese Seko's rule, the people lived in complete squalor. Still, Sese Seko brought some stability to the region. He ruled for 32 years, until the people finally rebelled in 1997.

Notice how conspicuous the second paragraph is. By allowing it to stand alone, the writer has made even clearer her emphasis on the cost of independence for the Republic of Congo.

▶ Practice 1

Divide the following text into paragraphs. Underline the topic sentence in each paragraph you create.

Sigmund Freud, the father of psychoanalysis, made many contributions to the science of psychology. One of his greatest contributions was his theory of the personality. According to Freud, the human personality is made up of three parts: the id, the ego, and the superego. The id is the part of the personality that exists only in the subconscious. According to Freud, the id has no direct contact with the reality. It is the innermost core of our personality and operates according to the pleasure principle. That is, it seeks immediate gratification for its desires, regardless of external realities or consequences. It is not even aware that external realities or consequences exist. The ego develops from the id and is the part of the personality in contact with the real world. The ego is conscious and therefore aims to satisfy the subconscious desire of the id as best it can within the individual's environment. When it can't satisfy those desires, it tried to control or suppress the id. The ego functions according to the reality principle. The superego is the third and final part of the personality to develop. This part of the personality contains our moral values and ideals, our notion of what's right and wrong. The superego gives us the "rules" that help the ego control the id. For example, a child wants a toy that belongs to another child (id). He checks his environment to see if it's possible to take that toy (ego). He can, and does. Then, he remembers that it's wrong to take something that belongs to someone else (superego) and returns the toy.

▶ Practice 2

On a separate piece of paper or on your computer, write topic sentences for the following paragraphs. Make at least one paragraph deductive (place the topic sentence at the beginning of the paragraph) and at least one paragraph inductive (place the topic sentence at the end of the paragraph).

1. The government's Bureau of Labor Statistics (BLS) reports that employment in child daycare services will grow over 300% in the next decade. In 2002, about 750,000 people worked in child daycare services. By 2012, that number is expected to be about 1,050,000—an increase of more than 300,000 jobs.

2. When I was in kindergarten, I wanted to be an astronaut. When I was in junior high school, I wanted to be a doctor. When I was in high school, I wanted to be a teacher. Today, I'm 35 and I'm a firefighter.

3. The proposed tax referendum will not reduce taxes for middle income families. In fact, middle income families with children will pay 10% more per year, and families without children will pay 20% more. Further, the referendum actually decreases taxes for the wealthiest tax bracket. In fact, taxpayers in the highest income bracket will pay 10% less per year if the referendum is passed.

▶ In Short

A paragraph is a group of sentences about one idea. That idea is typically expressed in a topic sentence. Deductive paragraphs begin with the topic sentence and then provide specific examples and evidence as support. Inductive paragraphs begin with the examples and evidence and then state the main idea in a topic sentence. Avoid long paragraphs, which are hard on the eye and often difficult to follow. Use one- or two-sentence paragraphs sparingly, to make an important idea stand out.

Skill Building until Next Time

Choose an essay from one of the collections suggested in the Additional Resources section at the end of the book, or a textbook you use in class. As you read, pay particular attention to paragraphing. When does the writer begin new paragraphs? Why? Can you identify the topic sentence? Do you recognize inductive or deductive formats?

10 ▶ Providing Support

LESSON SUMMARY

Your thesis is as important as the evidence that supports it. This lesson describes six different strategies for supporting your assertions.

In Lesson 1, the word *friendly* was used to describe the "general reader." It's important to think of your reader this way, because when you write for a friendly audience, you won't be tempted to employ an unnecessarily adversarial or defensive tone. But friendly doesn't mean that the reader will accept everything and anything you say. Unsubstantiated assertions will be questioned, and evidence will be required.

An essay is an explanation, not just of what you think, but of *why* you think it. The *why* comprises many types of support, including evidence, examples, and details. Most types of support are in one of six categories:

1. specific examples
2. facts
3. reasons
4. descriptions and anecdotes
5. expert opinion and analysis
6. quotations from the text

The boundaries of these categories are not absolute; an anecdote is often an example, and a reason can also be a fact. However, the categories are useful for discussing types of support and illustrating how to substantiate your assertions in a variety of ways.

▶ Specific Examples

Specific examples comprise the broadest category of evidence. Such an example offers something tangible to the reader; it is a person, place, or thing that exemplifies your idea. Let's examine the following statement:

Movies often portray the American suburb as a place of false happiness and hidden misery. But this is an unfair and inaccurate depiction.

This thesis has two ideas that need support: the portrayal of the American suburb as a place of false happiness and hidden misery, and that this depiction is unfair and inaccurate. You could cite films such as *American Beauty* and *The Ice Storm* as specific examples.

But examples can't simply be mentioned. To support your thesis, you'll need to demonstrate that both films portray the American suburb in precisely this negative way. You could begin this demonstration with a summary of the plot (remember, you shouldn't assume that a general reader has the same knowledge as you), and then offer the following specific examples as evidence:

- the Burnhams' home and neighborhood
- Mrs. Burnham's obsession with appearance
- the breakdown of the Burnhams' marriage
- Mr. Burnham's rebellion against the status quo
- Jane Burnham's hatred of her parents
- Mrs. Fitts' comatose state

Specific examples like these provide concrete evidence of your assertions. They make your claim "real" for your reader.

▶ Facts

The next form of support must be differentiated from opinion.

A **fact** is:
    something known for certain to have happened
    something known for certain to be true
    something known for certain to exist

An **opinion** is:

> something believed to have happened
> something believed to be true
> something believed to exist

Facts are what we know; they are *objective* and therefore do not change from person to person. Opinions are what we believe; they are *subjective* and debatable, and they often change from person to person. Because facts are objective, they're particularly valuable as evidence in an essay, especially when your thesis is controversial.

Facts include statistics, definitions, recorded statements, and observations. For example, a writer is drafting an essay assessing the flat tax from her outline (Lesson 6). Here is her thesis:

A flat tax would be good for the government and for citizens.

To support it, she could include the following facts:

- The IRS publishes 480 different tax forms.
- The IRB publishes 280 different tax forms to explain those 480 tax forms.
- The body of the tax law has 7.05 million words—ten times the number of words in the Bible.
- The cost of income tax compliance is over $1.3 billion a year (some sources estimate the cost as high as $2 billion).

▶ Practice 1

Choose one of the essays for which you developed an outline in Lesson 6 or 7. List at least four supporting ideas for your thesis. Include at least one specific example and at least one fact.

_____

_____

_____

_____

_____

A Note about Statistics

Statistics may seem like the most uncontestable kind of fact—after all, numbers are objective. But numbers can be, and often are, manipulated in many ways, including being taken out of context. Alert readers will want to see the source of your statistics to be sure the figures are unbiased. We'll explore this issue further in Lesson 11.

▶ Reasons

For many essays, the best way to support your thesis is to explain why you think the way you do. That explanation will lay out your reasons—some will be facts, others will be opinions. The key to this type of support is logic. Your reasons must be based on evidence or good common sense. That is, they must be logical.

To meet that standard, many reasons need considerable support. They can't simply be stated with an expectation that the audience will believe them. Here is another thesis:

School officials should not be allowed to randomly search students' lockers and backpacks.

For support, the following reasons could be used:

- These searches violate the right to privacy.
- Searches should not be done randomly, but only when there is a suspected violation.

Both of these reasons are opinions, and they need support to be convincing. The writer must use evidence to show that these opinions are logical and reasonable. To support the first reason, he could define the right to privacy (a combination of specific examples, facts, and description); he could provide an example or describe a certain situation where a search led to a violation of privacy (specific example, anecdote); and provide expert opinion.

To support the second assertion, he could explore the idea that "random searches" can lead to profiling of who is searched, and that without a suspected violation, everyone then becomes a suspect unless otherwise cleared of a violation; and provide expert opinion.

Of course, people's reasons for believing certain things are often very personal and highly debatable. While it's fine—and often effective—to use emotional arguments to convince your readers, the more logical your reasons, the more effective they will be as support.

▶ Description and Anecdotes

Evidence and support can also come in the form of short stories or descriptions that illustrate a point. Descriptions and anecdotes are effective evidence—especially in essays about people—because they help the reader form a picture that illuminates your ideas. In the following thesis, the writer addresses a college application essay topic:

The person I admire most is my sister. I call her Wonder Woman. A professional who copes daily with the most stressful and potentially depressing situations, she is the strongest person I know.

When writing a college application essay, remember that regardless of the topic, the essay needs to reveal something personal about *you*. Writing an essay about your sister in response to the prompt *"Indicate a person who has had a significant influence on you, and describe that influence"* is fine. However, you need to avoid the common pitfall of that prompt, which is to write about the person, and not about yourself. The writer of the sister essay needs to relate her sister's story to *herself*, not simply explain why her sister is the person she admires most.

The best kind of support for this essay will be description and anecdote—a series of "snapshots" and stories that illustrate the sister's strength. Here's an example:

Amy's job with the Division of Youth and Family Services is incredibly stressful. Every day for the past five years, she has visited families who are struggling with addiction, abuse, poverty, and hopelessness. One family has been "in the system" for a decade, cycling through the same problems without resolution. But instead of burning out, Amy's compassion and resolve have increased. She visits this family weekly, and is available to them almost 24 hours a day if a crisis arises. Once, she was awakened at three in the morning when the teenager in this family failed to come home. She got in her car and drove to their apartment, then called the police and helped them file a missing persons report. And this is just one family under her watch.

Similarly, to support the assertions that searches of students' lockers and backpacks should not be allowed, you could describe a search in which a student was unfairly accused and blamed for a crime. The following description appeared in a law journal article about such as case:

Wearing an orange prison jumpsuit and flip-flops, Sam Mazza looked dejected as he made his first court appearance. He was facing three years in prison for a crime he says was intended as a private joke. His spirits appeared to lift, however, when his attorney carefully laid out his case: The search of every locker in the school was unconstitutional. When Mazza's principal ordered the search, he was in violation of the "reasonable suspicion" component of legal searches. Since the note about a bomb threat (Mazza contends it was a joke) was found during an illegal search, the case had to be dropped. Mazza sat taller in his seat and smiled at his parents when his attorney concluded his remarks.

▶ Expert Opinion and Analysis

During a trial, lawyers often call upon *expert witnesses* to help them make their case. These witnesses were not involved in the crime, but they have expertise that can help the jurors determine the guilt or innocence of the defendant. Similarly, in many essays, and particularly in research papers, much of your support will come in the form of expert opinion and analysis. The experts you call upon can help you demonstrate the validity of your thesis.

You can collect expert opinion and analysis in two ways: by interviewing sources yourself (primary research) or by finding print or other recorded sources of expert opinion or analysis (secondary research). Sources of secondary research include the Internet, periodicals, journals, books, and transcripts.

The strength of expert opinion and analysis as evidence comes from the fact that your sources are experts. They've spend a great deal of time studying the issue or experiencing the phenomenon you're describing. In some cases, they know the issue far better that you or your readers do.

That's why you must give the credentials of any cited expert. It is not good to quote the author of *Jane Austen: The Ultimate Readers' Guide* on his opinions about *Pride and Prejudice* if you don't mention his book. This also helps avoid plagiarism. For another example, recall the flat tax essay. Its assertions could be supported with the following expert sources and their opinions:

- *Dr. Alan Auerbach, professor of Economics at the University of California of Berkeley and former chief economist at the Joint Committee on Taxation, estimates that the average family of four will have $3,000 more in income per year with a flat tax.*
- *The Tax Foundation, a nonprofit tax think tank, estimates that America spends $140 billion complying with the current tax code—a cost that would be reduced 94% by instituting a flat tax.*

Be certain to give enough identifying information about each expert source to convince your reader of the importance of his or her opinion.

▶ Quotations from the Text

When your essay is about literature, much of your evidence will come from the text itself. For example, imagine that you've written the following thesis statement:

In his poem "Splinter," Carl Sandburg uses metaphor and sound to suggest loss.

To support your assertion, you will need to discuss the poem's content, structure, and style. But that's only part of the task. In addition to telling the readers why you think what you do about the poem, you also need to show them the evidence that led you to your conclusion. Thus, you can tell readers that the poem suggests loss by the repetition of the short *i* sound, known as a phonetic intensive, in line 4 (thin, splinter, singing). You can also explain how metaphor is used to emphasize the same theme, and show evidence by quoting the last line, which describes the voice of the last cricket by comparing it to a thin splinter.

> *The voice of the last cricket*
> *across the first frost*
> *is one kind of good-by.*
> *It is so thin a splinter of singing.*

▶ Practice 2

Provide support for another essay outlined in Lesson 6 or 7, or add more support to the essay you used for Practice 1 in this lesson. List four supporting ideas, using at least two of the following types of evidence: reasons, descriptions or anecdotes, expert opinion and analysis, or quotations from the text.

_____

_____

_____

_____

_____

▶ In Short

Like lawyers in a courtroom trial, essay writers need to provide evidence for their assertions. That evidence can come in the form of specific examples, facts, reasons, descriptions and anecdotes, expert opinion and analysis, and quotations from the text.

Skill Building until Next Time

Read an opinion piece on the editorial page of today's newspaper. How does the author support his or her ideas? What kind of evidence does he or she provide? After you read the piece, keep it handy because you'll need to use it again in Lesson 11.

11 ▶ Strategies for Convincing

LESSON SUMMARY

While strong evidence is essential for an effective essay, it may not be enough to make your essay convincing. This lesson offers several strategies to help make your essays more persuasive.

Most essays are exercises in persuasive writing. You may want to persuade your reader to change his or her point of view, support a specific cause, or agree with your opinion. In an SAT or ACT essay, your goal is to convince the scorer that you can write well. For a college application, your essay needs to persuade the admissions officer to accept you. On a more general level, because essays are built on the assertion → support structure, your underlying goal is to convince your readers that your thesis is valid.

The best way to convince readers that your thesis is valid is to provide strong and sufficient support. However, support alone is not always enough. The way in which you present your evidence, though, can mean the difference between a successfully persuasive essay, and one that is easily dismissed. Here are six strategies that work with your supporting evidence to make your essays more convincing:

1. Be specific.
2. Don't include ideas you can't support.
3. Establish credibility.
4. Acknowledge counterarguments.
5. Avoid absolutes.
6. Don't offend.

▶ Be Specific

Whatever your topic or assignment, the more precise you are throughout your essay, the easier it will be for your readers to accept your assertions. Specific examples and details make abstract ides concrete, and something that's clear and concrete is more easily accepted than something vague and abstract.

For example, look at the difference between the next two paragraphs. The first lacks specific examples and details and therefore lacks persuasive power. The second paragraph, however, offers some very specific examples and details. It is much more convincing than its vague counterpart is.

To confirm my hypothesis, I asked my peers about the balance between work and play. Most of them said they thought the balance should be about equal. Several of them pointed out that because of technology, the distinction between work and home is fading, so it's especially important to set aside time for play.

To confirm my hypothesis, I interviewed 30 of my peers—students from both the public and private high schools in my area. I asked, "What do you think is the right relationship between work and play?" Twenty-two respondents said they think work and play should have equal time in our lives. "We should play at least as much as we work," said Ellen Reese, a senior planning to major in computer science. "Of course, that's a lot easier to do if you love your job, because then that's part of the play, too." Andrew Fry, a junior who wants to be a journalist, was one of the 12 respondents concerned with the collapsing distinction between work and home. "Between e-mail and the Internet, wireless connections, and cell phones, we can take our work with us anywhere and work any time of the day. So many people bring their work home with them and let it eat up their play time. I think it's really important to set aside time each day, or at least each week, to relax and play."

Notice how the writer of the second paragraph offers specific information: the number of students polled, the kind of students polled, and the exact question she asked them. This gives the reader a much clearer sense of her survey and helps him or her better understand the results. Then, instead of generalizing the responses, she offers more specifics, such as exactly how many students felt there should be an equal balance. Importantly, she also offers specific responses. She doesn't just tell us what people said by paraphrasing; she shows us by quoting their responses. Once again, abstract ideas and generalizations are made more concrete—and therefore more convincing.

▶ If You Can't Support It, Don't Include It

Imagine you're on a jury. The prosecuting attorney turns to the jury box and says, "The defendant is clearly guilty. I just know it." He doesn't offer any evidence to support his assertion. Absurd, of course. No legitimate lawyer working in her client's best interest would make such a claim if she weren't able to support it. The rule is *if you can't support it, don't include it*, and it is as important for writers as it is for attorneys.

For example, you might believe that Americans today work more hours and have less leisure time than at any other time in our history. There are probably statistics out there to support this assertion, but after a quick search on the Internet, you find nothing. Unless you're willing to put in more research time to find what you need, as strongly as you may feel about the idea, since you can't support it, you shouldn't include it.

That doesn't mean you have to scrap the idea altogether, though. If you can't find evidence for the claim that Americans in general work more and play less than ever before, you might be able to find evidence that supports the assertion on a smaller scale. For many types of essays, you don't need the kind of evidence that's only found though research. Personal examples supported with specific examples can work if your assignment isn't a formal research paper. You could rework your assertion by reducing its scope and stating the following:

These days, everyone in my family is working more than ever—both at home and at the office.

By using specific personal examples, facts, and anecdotes, this type of assertion can have a legitimate place in your essay.

▶ Establish Credibility

Credibility is the quality of being trustworthy and believable. The more credible a person is, the more likely you are to accept his or her opinions as valid (well founded, logical). As a writer, you need to establish credibility on two levels: your own credibility and the credibility of your sources.

Credibility is built upon two factors: *expertise* and freedom from *bias*. A **bias** is an opinion or feeling that strongly favors one side over others. **Expertise** is established by education, experience, job or position, reputation, and achievements. In general, the greater the expertise and the lower the potential for bias, the greater the credibility.

The Credibility of Your Sources

As mentioned in Lesson 10, when you use expert opinion or analysis to support your assertions, it's important to let readers know who your sources are and what the nature of their expertise is. Of course, you don't have room to include extensive biographies or resumes of each source, but some basic information can establish their authority. If your source is a person, include his or her title, affiliation (does he or she work for a recognized or renowned organization or institution of higher learning?), and a major achievement or two. If your source is an organization, let readers know something about its history and achievements. For example, let's look again at the expert sources used for the flat tax essay:

- *Dr. Alan Auerbach, professor of Economics at the University of California of Berkeley and former chief economist at the Joint Committee on Taxation, estimates that the average family of four will have $3,000 more in income per year with a flat tax.*

- *The Tax Foundation, a nonprofit tax think tank, estimates that America spends $140 billion complying with the current tax code—a cost that would be reduced 94% by instituting a flat tax.*

In the first example, the writer tells readers Dr. Auerbach's current and former positions, both of which demonstrate that he is an expert on the subject of taxes. In the second example, the title of the organization—The Tax Foundation—tells readers that the organization is devoted to the subject. The writer describes it as a "think tank," which suggests that it seeks out and employs experts on the subject.

Determining Bias

While every author, like every person, has opinions about most subjects, authors of factual information are often assumed to be without such bias. Bias in this context refers to a preference that makes one prejudiced. Newspaper and television reporters, for example, are expected to deliver the facts without offering an opinion. However, you should never assume a lack of bias.

For example, the 24-hour cable news channel, Fox News, uses the phrase *fair and balanced* to describe its coverage. However, many critics have accused the channel of being biased. Try watching and reading the news from a variety of sources. Check for differences in story coverage: Who spent more time on the four-alarm fire than on the orphanage story? Who skipped the orphanage story to cover more of a politician's handshaking opportunities that day? You may also be interested in finding out more about the reporters and commentators who deliver the news. Are they former politicians, or political speechwriters? Do they have affiliations with special interest groups? What, if any, are their biases?

These sources then, have expertise. But that doesn't mean they're credible. Many seemingly knowledgeable and trustworthy sources are actually incorrect or biased. In order to trust the source of any information, you need to determine the agenda of the person/organization disseminating it. Are they simply trying to relay facts, or are they trying to get you to believe something, or change your mind on a subject? It can be difficult to find a direct answer to that question, but you can begin to get a clearer picture by looking into the following:

- What are the author's credentials on this subject?

Is he or she qualified to write on the topic based on background or education? For some subjects, it is acceptable to use information obtained from a hobbyist, self-proclaimed expert, or enthusiast, if you can verify it elsewhere. However, you should obtain most information from a reputable source. And since you need to verify anyway, why not use information, for instance, derived from Yale University's Thomas Hardy Association, rather than from John Doe's personal website homage to his favorite writer, Hardy?

- Does the author document sources?

Where do relevant facts and figures come from? If you are consulting print material, there should be footnotes and a bibliography that show the author's sources. On the Internet, you may also find such documentation, or sources may be documented by using links to other websites (see the following section on evaluating a website based on links). Even documentaries, to use a previous example, should cite sources in their credits.

- Are the sources balanced and reputable?

Pages of footnotes are meaningless if they simply indicate that the author used untrustworthy sources him- or herself. Check some of the sources to verify that they are accurate and unbiased. For example, a book on gun laws that relies heavily on material published by the National Rifle Association is not as reliable a source as another book on the subject that uses a wide variety of sources representing both sides of the issue.

■ What do others say about the author (whether individual or group)?

A quick way to check for opinions is to "Google" the author. Simply put his or her name (or the name of the group if there is no individual author) in the search box in quotes. The results can be revealing. However, remember to read them with a critical eye. If you are searching for someone with a radical or controversial view, you'll probably find detractors. A handful shouldn't deter you, but pages of negative information might.

Your Own Credibility

The best way to establish your expertise is to demonstrate to readers that you've "done your homework"—that is, that you've considered issues carefully and consulted the research, if necessary, to support your position. To show your audience that you are not unfairly biased, you'll also need to acknowledge counterarguments and make concessions. These two strategies are explained in the sections that follow.

▶ Practice 1

You've been given an essay assignment about the impact of violence on television. Following are two "facts" and their sources. Create a brief profile of each source to make that source credible. Then, for each "fact," write a sentence that includes the fact, its source, and enough information about the source to establish credibility.

"Fact" 1: The average television channel shows 579 acts of violence in a 24-hour period.
Source: Emily Rhodes
Profile:

_____

_____

_____

Sentence:

_____

_____

"Fact" 2: Violent crimes committed by juveniles have quadrupled since 1973.
Source: Children's Watch
Profile:

_____

_____

_____

Sentence:

_____

_____

▶ Acknowledge Counterarguments

An important part of establishing your credibility and persuading readers is acknowledging counterarguments. Counterarguments are ones that might be offered by someone supporting the other side of your argument. If you are asserting that medical research on animals is unnecessary, you need to consider what someone asserting that it is necessary would think.

Acknowledging counterarguments strengthens your argument. It shows that you have considered all sides of the issue and thought carefully about the logic of your position. More importantly, it helps you better defend your position. If you know what objections your readers might have, you can systematically address those objections in your essay (without, in many cases, revealing them as possible objections). Furthermore, acknowledging counterarguments enables you to persuade your readers to believe you by addressing their concerns and then countering each concern with a reasonable premise of your own.

Compare these two arguments:

Lukas, can I borrow your car tomorrow morning? I have a job interview and I can't get there by bus. I really want this job. What do you say?

Lukas, I know you don't like to let other people drive your car, especially since you put so much time into rebuilding it. But I'm hoping you'll make an exception. I have a job interview tomorrow and I can't get there by bus. I'm really excited about this job. I promise to have it back by noon with a full tank of gas. And to show my appreciation, I'll take her to the car wash on my way back.

It's clear that the speaker in the second paragraph took some time to consider Lukas's point of view. By addressing his concerns, the writer shows Lukas that he's put himself in Lukas's shoes, and this kind of empathy can be a powerful tool for convincing a reader.

To help you acknowledge counterarguments, play "devil's advocate." While brainstorming or outlining, take a few minutes to consider the opposite thesis; how would it best be supported? What arguments would likely be made? If you can anticipate what the other side will say, you can acknowledge those arguments and come up with effective counterarguments. It will also help you find any holes in your argument that you may have missed.

Acknowledging counterarguments is not the same as supporting them. In fact, if you acknowledge them strategically, you can actually use them to support your case. For example, you are arguing that school uniforms should be mandatory for all public school students. One of your major supporting ideas is that school uniforms will create a stronger sense of community. After playing devil's advocate, you realize that people against the idea of mandatory uniforms would argue that they create a culture of conformity. Here's how you might acknowledge the counterargument, show its weakness, and set the reader up for your position:

Many people have argued that school uniforms would encourage conformity, and that schools should do all they can to help students develop a sense of individuality. But as much as we want to believe that the way we dress is an expression of our individuality, for most students, clothing is more often a means of conformity. Students want to dress like their peers. They want to wear the same brands and the same styles as their friends (or the people whom they wish were their friends). It is the rare student who truly uses clothing as an expression of individuality.

Now that the writer has addressed the counterargument, he can go on to develop his position—that school uniforms will create a sense of community.

▶ Practice 2

You are writing an essay on the subject of censorship on the Internet. Take a stance on this issue and write a brief thesis statement on a separate sheet of paper or on your computer. Then, come up with three supporting points. Next, play devil's advocate and list three points the opposition might make. Finally, write a brief paragraph in which you acknowledge one of those points.

▶ Avoid Absolutes

Persuasive writing involves pitting one side against another—and showing why one side is superior. It's easy to fall into the trap of thinking in terms of black and white. If one side is correct, that means the other side is wrong, right? When you write in terms of absolutes, especially *all* or *none*, you weaken your writing. There are always exceptions, and a good essay is one that's careful to avoid statements that don't allow for those exceptions. Most absolutes are gross generalizations or stereotypes, both of which you need to avoid.

Failure to acknowledge exceptions will seriously undermine your credibility with your reader. Here's an example:

Little Red Riding Hood is portrayed as naïve and innocent, just like all girls in fairy tales.

Well, maybe in all the fairy tales *you've* read, but in fact, many fairy tales describe girls who are sophisticated, cunning, and even dangerous. There are many exceptions to the "rule" this writer just established, and thoughtful readers will be put off by such a statement.

To allow for exceptions, exchange absolutes for less restrictive words and phrases. A single word such as *many* or *most* can change a problematic, implausible absolute into a plausible, provable statement. Here are some of those exchanges:

INSTEAD OF "ALL," SAY:	INSTEAD OF "NONE," SAY:
most	almost none
many	very few
just about all/just about every	with few exceptions
nearly all	only a handful
the majority of	some

The fairy tale statement could be revised as follows:

Little Red Riding Hood is portrayed as naïve and innocent, like many girls in fairy tales.

▶ Don't Offend

If you want to successfully persuade your audience, don't offend them. Students often don't realize that something they've written may be offensive—but that's usually because they have a very specific reader in mind. That is, they imagine a general reader who has a lot more in common with them than a true general reader might. This kind of thinking can produce statements such as:

All people who claim to believe in the existence of alien life forms are simply unable to distinguish between fact and opinion.

Besides being an absolute (suggesting that *all* people who claim to believe in alien life forms can't distinguish between fact and opinion), this claim is insulting to those who believe that some kind of alien life does exist on other planets. You may believe that the existence of extraterrestrial life is an invalid theory, but many people (including some very highly regarded scientists) do not. If your reader happens to believe that we are not alone in the universe, he or she probably won't take your arguments seriously (no matter how strong they might be), because he or she has been offended. Even if your audience is made up of those who share your opinions, they're likely to bristle at your insensitivity, and as a result, you'll lose credibility in their eyes as well.

▶ In Short

Writers use many strategies to make their essay more convincing. They provide specific details to make ideas more concrete, they establish credibility and acknowledge counterarguments, they don't include assertions they can't support, they avoid absolutes, and they take care not to offend their audience.

Skill Building until Next Time

Look at the essay you read for **Skill Building until Next Time** in the previous lesson. What strategies for convincing do you see at work? Does the essay include many specific details? Does the writer establish credibility? How? Does he or she acknowledge counterarguments? How? Note the number of different strategies used in the essay.

12 ▶ Introductions

LESSON SUMMARY

First impressions are important. This lesson explains the purpose of introductions and how to write a "hook" that grabs the reader's attention.

Right or wrong, in the business world, many decisions are based solely on first impressions. Companies spend thousands, and even millions, in advertising dollars to make sure your first impression of them is a good one.

First impressions are just as important in writing. A college admissions officer who's reading his fortieth essay of the day will probably put it down if it begins, "In this essay, I will . . ." If you tell him in the first few sentences what you will say in the next dozens, what is his incentive to continue? If you begin a science lab report with the specifics of an experiment, your teacher will probably give it a poor grade.

Both of these are examples of students who don't understand the purpose and power of an introduction. While it can vary slightly from one type of writing assignment to another, the introduction is a critical part of the essay, and if it's not included, it can ruin what might otherwise be a well-written piece.

▶ What an Introduction Should Do

A combination of courtesy and strategy, the introduction "sells" the essay to the reader, compelling him or her to read the rest of it. For most assignments, it should also acquaint the audience with the subject and purpose of the essay. Specifically, essay writers have four tasks to accomplish within the first paragraph or two. An effective introduction should:

1. **Provide the context necessary to understand your thesis.** When you're writing for a general audience, your readers don't know who you are. They may not know your assignment and may not be familiar with the issues or texts you are discussing. Thus, you might need to provide background information. If you are writing about literature, you should include the titles, authors, and publications dates of the text you are analyzing. Similarly, if you're writing about a historical event, you should name the event, the date, and the key people (or countries, or issues) involved. Here's an example:

   Mary Shelley's novel Frankenstein *was published over 180 years ago. But this remarkable novel raises a question that is more important today than ever: What is a creator's responsibility for his or her creation?*

2. **Clearly state the main point of the essay.** Your readers should know from the beginning what idea you will be developing throughout the essay. A clear thesis statement is a key component of an effective introduction. (See Lesson 9 for a review of thesis statements.) In the previous example, the last sentence expresses the main idea of the essay—the question, and its relevance today.

   The exception to this rule is the college application essay. Because of the high volume of essays each admissions officer must read, it makes sense to stand out, and keep his or her attention, by being mysterious in your introduction. Make him or her read on to the second paragraph by not revealing your subject until then.

   Here's an example:

   I will never forget the moment I landed in Rio de Janeiro, Brazil. As the plane descended, I was awed by the dynamic geography and the juxtaposition of the sea, the mountains, and the city's skyline. I absorbed the landscape further and my eyes focused on the favelas mounted on the hillsides.

   This introduction works well on a number of levels: It takes the reader to an exotic location, describing the landscape and setting the scene. The writer tells you the moment is unforgettable, and brings you along with her. But, most importantly, she does not reveal anything about her subject. You have to read on to find out what her essay is about.

3. **"Hook" the reader.** The introduction should not only get the reader's attention, but compel him or her to keep reading. The next section examines some of the many ways to write a successful hook.

4. **Set the tone for the essay.** Tone refers to the mood or attitude conveyed through language, particularly through word choice and sentence structure. Your tone may be personal and informal, serious and formal, urgent, relaxed, grave, or humorous. In the *Frankenstein* example, the language is serious and formal, and it fits the serious subject (supporting examples in the essay include discussions of atomic weapons and cloning).

▶ Ways to Grab Your Reader's Attention

A good hook contains an element of creativity and an awareness of the reader's needs. It doesn't simply announce the subject or thesis, or make generalizations that sound clichéd. Phrases such as *one step at a time; no news is good news; have a nice day; when life gives you lemons, make lemonade; and no guts, no glory* are so overused they have little or no meaning.

The following seven introductory hook strategies offer specific ways to get into your subject and thesis that arouse a reader's attention, making your introduction an invitation to read on. These strategies are:

1. a quotation
2. a question
3. a surprising statement or fact
4. an imaginary situation or scenario
5. an anecdote
6. interesting background information
7. a new twist on a familiar phrase

A Quotation
Start with a quote from a text, a film, a subject-matter expert, or even a friend or relative if he or she said something relevant to the topic and of interest to your reader.

"All animals are equal, but some animals are more equal than others," said Napoleon in George Orwell's classic novel Animal Farm. *Uncle Sam might say something similar: "All people must pay taxes, but some must pay more taxes than others." Our current federal income tax system treats taxpayers unfairly and requires and monumental budget to administer and maintain. A flat tax, which would treat all taxpayers equally and dramatically reduce tax compliance cost, is the answer.*

A Question
Open up with a question to get your readers thinking. Of course, the question (and its answer) should be relevant to your thesis.

What's in a name? Nothing—and everything. It is, after all, just a name, one tiny piece of the puzzle that makes up a person. But when someone has a nickname like "Dumbo," a name can be the major force in shaping one's sense of self. That's how it was for me.

A Surprising Statement or Fact

This type of hook provides "shock value" for the reader.

If you don't believe our current tax law is ridiculously out of control, consider this: Our total tax law consists of 101,295 pages and 7.05 million words. That means our tax law has almost 100 times more pages and ten times as many words and the Bible. Bloated? You bet. But it doesn't have to be. The government would collect equal or greater tax revenue and save millions of dollars in compliance costs by instituting a flat tax system.

▶ Practice 1

On a separate sheet of paper or on your computer, write an introductory hook for one of the essays you brainstormed or outlined in an earlier lesson. Use a quotation, a question, or a surprising statement or fact.

An Imaginary Situation or Scenario

Hook your readers with your imagination. You might ask them to place themselves in the scene, or you can let them simply witness it.

You've been drifting at sea for days with no food and no water. You have two companions. Suddenly, a half-empty bottle of water floats by. You fight over the bottle, ready to kill the others if you have to for that water. What has happened? What are you—human or animal? It is a question that H.G. Wells raises over and over in The Island of Dr. Moreau. *His answer? Like it or not, we're both.*

An Anecdote

Start your essay by telling a short, interesting story related to your subject.

I'd been getting into a lot of trouble—failing classes, taking things that didn't belong to me. So the guidance counselor at school suggested that my parents take me to a psychiatrist. "You mean a shrink?" my mother replied, horrified. My father and I had the same reaction. After all, what good would it do to lie on a couch while some "doctor" asked questions and took notes? So I went to my first session angry and skeptical. But after a few weeks, I realized that we had it all wrong. Those shrinks really know what they're doing. And mine helped me turn my life around.

Another Word about College Application Essays

You're writing not only to show off your writing skills, but also to sell yourself to the admissions officer (your reader). It doesn't make sense to reveal unflattering or potentially damaging information about yourself. It is the reader's job to select candidates who are not only smart enough, but also emotionally stable enough to stay in school and do well for four years. They'll probably reject you if you give them reason to believe you might not be able to handle college. While the hook of the essay about seeing a psychiatrist is well done, it's not the kind of material that works for the application essay.

Interesting Background Information

Tell your reader something unusual about your subject. Here's a revision of the *Frankenstein* introduction using this strategy:

Incredibly, Frankenstein—one of the most important novels in Western literature—was written by a teenager. When it was published in 1818, Mary Shelley was only 19 years old. Despite her youth, Shelley's story raises a question that is more important today that ever: What is the creator's relationship to his or her creation?

A New Twist on a Familiar Phrase

Reword or rework an old standard to create a fresh hook.

To eat or not to eat? That is the question millions of Americans struggle with every day as they fight the battle of the bulge. But it seems to be a losing battle. Despite the millions spent on diet pills and diet plans, Americans today are heavier than ever.

There are many reasons for this nationwide weight gain, but experts agree that the main cause is lack of exercise. And one of the reasons we don't get enough exercise is because we spend too much time in front of the TV.

Notice that this introduction is actually two paragraphs. In some essays, the introduction runs three or even four paragraphs. The key is to have an introduction that is in proportion with the rest of the essay. If your essay is two pages long, one paragraph is probably sufficient for the introduction. If it goes longer, the body of your essay, where you develop your main points and support them with evidence and examples, will lack the room it needs to completely state your case. But if your essay is ten or twelve pages long, it may take a couple of paragraphs to properly introduce your topic and thesis. You might have a more detailed anecdote, for example, or spend two or three paragraphs describing a scenario that sets up your thesis.

▶ Practice 2

Write a two-paragraph introduction for one of the essay examples provided in the first half of this book. Use one of these strategies: an imaginary situation or scenario, an anecdote, interesting background information, or a new twist on a familiar phrase.

▶ In Short

Introductions serve an important function. They "welcome" your reader into your essay by providing context, stating your thesis, and setting the tone. They should also grab your reader's interest. Strategies for attention-grabbing hooks include starting with a quotation, a question, a surprising statement or fact, an imaginary situation or scenario, an anecdote, interesting background information, or a new twist on a familiar phrase.

Skill Building until Next Time

Skim through a magazine, reading only the introductions to the articles. What techniques do writers use to grab your interest? Do the introductions provide context and state the main point of the article? What tone do they set for the rest of the essay?

13 ▶ Conclusions

LESSON SUMMARY

How you conclude your essay is just as important as how you introduce it. This lesson will explain what conclusions should do and how to write an ending that has impact.

Have you ever enjoyed a movie only to be disappointed by its ending? Though the ending may be just a small fraction of the movie's length, if it's not satisfying, it can ruin the whole experience. The same is often true for essays. A powerful conclusion can dramatically improve a reader's impression of a weak or mediocre essay, while a weak conclusion can do the reverse, leaving a bad impression of an otherwise well-written essay.

▶ What a Conclusion Should Do

Like the introduction, the conclusion of an essay serves a specific function. Its job is to wrap things up in a way that makes readers feel satisfied with their reading experience. Writers create this sense of satisfaction by:

1. restating the thesis in different words
2. offering a new understanding
3. providing a sense of closure
4. arousing the reader's emotions

Restating the Thesis

Before your reader finishes your essay, remind him or her of what your goals were. What did you want him or her to take away from your essay? Reminding readers of your thesis (without repeating it word for word) will help ensure that they get, and remember, your point.

Introduction: *What's in a name? Nothing—and everything. It is, after all, just a name, one tiny piece of the puzzle that makes up a person. But when someone has a nickname like "Dumbo," a name can be the major force in shaping one's sense of self. That's how it was for me.*

Conclusion: *I don't blame my brother for how I turned out, of course. He may have given me the nickname, but I'm the one who let that nickname determine how I felt about myself. I could have worn the name proudly—after all, Disney's Dumbo is a hero. Instead, I wore it like a dunce cap. I wish I had known then what I know now: You are what you believe yourself to be.*

Offering a New Understanding

To conclude means *to bring to an end*. But it also means *to arrive at a belief or opinion by reasoning*. And that's what a good conclusion should do: It should both bring the essay to an end *and* end with a conclusion—the understanding that you have come to by working through your essay. After all, you stated a thesis and then supported it with evidence. That has to add up to something. You should now have a deeper understanding of your subject, and it's this understanding that you need to convey to your readers in your conclusion. This understanding makes readers feel as if their time was well spent; it is their "reward" for reading your essay.

In the previous example, the writer offers a new understanding of how names can shape people. Readers learn that he had the choice to let the nickname shape him in a positive or negative way. The understanding is his "gift" to his readers, and he shares it in his conclusion.

Providing a Sense of Closure

Good conclusions often offer a new understanding, but that new understanding is very closely related to the thesis. The conclusion is not the time to introduce a new topic. Don't bring up assertions that have not already been supported by the body of your essay. Doing so will not only frustrate your reader, but will probably cause him or her to lose sight of your thesis. In the following examples, one conclusion provides closure while offering a new understanding, while the other one goes off on a tangent unrelated to the original thesis.

I don't blame my brother for how I turned out, of course. He may have given me the nickname, but I'm the one who let that nickname determine how I felt about myself. I could have worn the name proudly—after all, Disney's Dumbo is a hero. Instead, I wore it like a dunce cap. I wish I had known then what I know now: You are what you believe yourself to be.

The Word *Conclude* Means:

1. *to bring to an end*
2. *to arrive at a belief or opinion by reasoning*

I don't blame my brother for how I turned out, of course. He may have given me the nickname, but I'm the one who let that nickname determine how I felt about myself. I could have worn the name proudly—after all, Disney's Dumbo is a hero. Disney knew what he was doing when he created the Dumbo character—he's someone most of us can relate to, and he has a lot to teach children.

Even without reading the body of the essay, it is evident that the last sentence of the second conclusion doesn't relate closely to the thesis. The writer leaves his reader with thoughts about a movie and its creator, and not about his nickname and how it affected his sense of self. The first conclusion is successful because it maintains close ties with the thesis, even as it draws a new conclusion, or gives a new understanding, about that thesis.

The Art of Framing

One of the most effective ways to provide a sense of closure is to "frame" your essay with a conclusion that refers to the introduction. The introduction and conclusion use the same approach, presented in different terms. The conclusion then serves as a reminder of where the essay began.

In the sample conclusions offered later in this lesson, notice how the "anecdote" conclusion frames the *Dumbo* essay by repeating the opening question and providing a more sophisticated answer. Similarly, the "call to action" conclusion frames the *To eat or not to eat?* essay by referring to the essay's opening lines.

Arousing the Reader's Emotions

Good conclusions can also move readers by appealing to their emotions. Because your conclusion restates and extends your thesis by offering a new understanding, and because you want your essay to end with impact, it makes sense to write a memorable ending. One of the best ways to do that is through emotion. The conclusion to the *Dumbo* essay, for example, touches our emotions by making us think about how we may have let negative beliefs about ourselves dictate who we have become. At the same time, it inspires us by suggesting that we have the power to change ourselves if we have a negative self-image.

▶ Strategies for Conclusions

Just as there are many strategies for creating an attention-getting introduction, there are a number of strategies for creating a powerful conclusion. These are among the most effective:

- a quotation
- an anecdote
- a prediction
- a solution or recommendation
- a call to action

A Quotation

You may have noticed that three of the introduction strategies we discussed in the previous lesson—quotations, questions, and anecdotes—are also effective for conclusions. Here's how you might use a quotation to sum up an essay:

In Grand Illusion, the whole idea of nationhood is exposed as an illusion, and the fact that we go to war over an illusion is the film's greatest irony—and tragedy. It is a tragedy Renoir hopes we can avoid repeating. If "losing an illusion makes you wiser than finding the truth," as Ludwig Borne wrote, then Renoir has succeeded in making us all more wise.

A Question

Here's how you might use a question to conclude an essay:

"What kind of place is America?" you asked. In short, America is an idea and an experiment. We call the idea "democracy," and we see what happens when we let people say whatever they want, go wherever they want, and in most cases, do whatever they want. True, the results aren't always pretty. But it certainly is a beautiful experiment, isn't it?

An Anecdote

Anecdotes add interest and impact to conclusions. Notice how this anecdote frames the essay by repeating the question used in the introduction.

Introduction: What's in a name? Nothing—and everything. It is, after all, just a name, one tiny piece of the puzzle that makes up a person. But when someone has a nickname like "Dumbo," a name can be the major force in shaping one's sense of self. That's how it was for me.

Conclusion: What's in a name? Enough to make me think long and hard about what to name my son before he was born. I spent months researching names and their meanings and thinking about the nicknames people might come up with. Once we finally settled on a name, I spent many sleepless nights worrying that we'd made the wrong choice and petrified that Samuel James would hate us for giving him that name. But I've realized that along the way, Sam will have to learn the same lesson I did. I only hope that I can help make it less painful.

▶ Practice 1

On a separate sheet of paper or on your computer, write a conclusion for an introduction you wrote in Lesson 12. Use one of the following strategies to frame the essay: quotation, question, or anecdote.

A Prediction

You can close your essay with a forecast for a person, place, or thing related to your thesis. Here's an example from a college application essay:

Thirty years from now, when I'm 48, I will retire and survey my empire. I will have created and led a hugely successful Fortune 500 company; I will have used my considerable wealth to set up a literacy foundation and a home for orphans in my native Cuba. Deeply satisfied with my accomplishments, I will then establish scholarships for disadvantaged students to Briarwood College, for I will recall with great gratitude that my education there made all of my accomplishments possible.

A Solution or Recommendation

Conclude with a solution to the problem you've discussed, or a recommendation for future action. This strategy will serve you well later, when you're asked to write business memos or reports. Here is a conclusion from an essay that examines misinformation on the Internet:

While the Internet can be a very valuable source of information, it contains so much misinformation that it's almost criminal. Though we can't—and shouldn't—regulate what people put up on the Web, we can—and should—provide guidelines for citizens surfing the Web. Why not create a "reliability index" that measures the trustworthiness of websites? Then the Web can truly be what it was meant to be: an asset, and not a liability.

A Call to Action

Finally, you can end your essay by suggesting a specific action that your readers should take. As with the solution or recommendation strategy, this one is also used often in business writing. Here's an example of a conclusion for the essay about television and lack of exercise. Notice how it frames the essay by referring to the opening line of the introduction.

Introduction: *To eat or not to eat? That is the question millions of Americans struggle with every day as they fight the battle of the bulge. But it seems to be a losing battle. Despite the millions spent on diet pills and diet plans, Americans today are heavier than ever.*

There are many reasons for this nationwide weight gain, but experts agree that the main cause is lack of exercise. And one of the reasons we don't get enough exercise is because we spend too much time in front of the TV.

Conclusion: *Television entertains and informs us. But it also fattens us. If you are one of the millions of overweight Americans, take a simple step toward a healthier body. Get up and turn off the TV. The question isn't "To eat or not to eat." Rather, the question is, what can you do instead of watching TV? Go for a walk. Take a swim. Ride a bike. Get some exercise! You'll end up with a healthier body—and mind.*

▶ Practice 2

On a separate sheet of paper or on your computer, write a conclusion for the other introduction you wrote for Lesson 12. Use one of the following strategies: a prediction, solution or recommendation, or call to action.

▶ In Short

Like introductions, conclusions serve several important functions. They refocus the essay by restating the thesis; they offer a gift to the reader in the form of a new understanding (which is an extension of the thesis); they provide a sense of closure; and they arouse readers' emotions. Some of the same strategies for introductions also work for conclusions, including quotations, questions, and anecdotes. Other closing techniques include predictions, solutions or recommendations, and calls to action.

Skill Building until Next Time

Skim through a magazine, but this time, read the introductions and conclusion to at least three articles. What techniques do writers use to conclude their articles? Do the conclusions restate the main idea or thesis offered in the introduction? Do they go a step further and offer a new understanding? Do they provide a sense of closure? Do they speak to your emotions? What techniques do the writers use to conclude their articles?

SECTION

3 ▶

Revising, Editing, and Proofreading the Essay

ONCE YOU HAVE a rough draft of your essay, you are ready to transform it into a polished piece of writing. This polishing process consists of three steps: revising, editing, and proofreading. Think of them as holding up various strengths of magnifying glasses to your essay:

- **Revising** looks at your essay through a lens that lets you see it as a whole; you will pay attention to the largest issues involved in its crafting. Have you addressed the topic? Is there a logical flow to your ideas or story? Is each paragraph necessary and properly placed?
- **Editing** takes a closer look at your writing, through a stronger lens that highlights words and sentences. Are your word choices appropriate and fresh? Are there any repetitive or awkward sentences or phrases?
- **Proofreading** puts your essay under the strongest lens. You will check *within* each word for errors in spelling and correct any other mechanical mistakes, such as grammar and punctuation.

14 ▶ Revising: The Big Picture

LESSON SUMMARY

This is the first of two lessons dealing with the revision process. It shows you how to revise for three important "big picture" issues: fulfilling the assignment, stating a clear thesis, and providing strong support.

From the Latin *revisere*, meaning to visit or look at again, revision is the most general re-examination of your essay. But it can also seem like the most overwhelming; it's harder to step back and look at your entire essay with fresh eyes and ears than it is to correct spelling and punctuation errors. But this is a critical step in which you make sure you have achieved your goal, and see if any sections of the essay need improving.

Revision takes place on a couple of levels: the "big picture" or essay level, and the paragraph level. It makes sense to look at your writing on these levels first, before jumpig into editing or proofreading. Think of it this way: Why take the time to correct grammatical errors and reword sentences if you might delete those sentences later in the revision process?

▶ Re-visioning

You can look at your essay with "fresh eyes" in two ways—literally, by giving your work to a trusted reader for feedback, and figuratively, by examining your own work as if you've never seen it before.

If you think professional writers work alone, think again. They know how important it is to get feedback before they send their work to the publisher—it's not uncommon for them to share their work with a number of trusted readers first. That strategy is important for your essays, too. Readers can help you pinpoint the strengths and weaknesses of your writing. They can tell you what works well, and what doesn't; what comes across clearly to them, and what confuses them.

When you share your writing with people you trust to give you honest feedback, ask them:

- What do you like about my essay?
- Is there anything that seems confusing or unclear?
- What do you think my purpose was in writing this essay?
- Is there anything you need to know more about, or that needs more explanation?
- What do you think I could do to improve this essay?

These questions can also work when you direct them to yourself. But before you reread for revising, take a break. The best revisions take place a day or two after you've completed your draft. That time lets you approach your work with the "fresh eyes" we mentioned earlier in this lesson.

Try reading your essay aloud. Read as if you are presenting it to an audience, and listen to your words. This technique can help you find places where your wording sounds awkward, or where your sentences are confusing or too long. You can also hear where your writing simply doesn't convey what you intended it to. Mark those areas that sound as if they should be revised, making notes of ideas for how to improve them. Remember to keep in mind the following:

- Does my essay fulfill the assignment?
- Is my thesis statement clear? Is it easily identifiable?
- Are my ideas well supported with examples, evidence, and details?

Reworking

Once you've got feedback and have taken your own notes on what could be improved, it's time to make changes. Those changes could be additions, deletions, or rewordings. The second type of change is probably the hardest. Especially if you don't consider yourself a strong writer, you may feel unwilling to give up a paragraph, or even a sentence. But revising is about keeping what works, and fixing or eliminating what doesn't. If it doesn't work, it detracts from the rest of your essay and needs to go.

Fulfilling the Assignment

On the largest scale, if your draft doesn't fulfill the requirements of the assignment, you need to figure out where you went wrong. You probably don't need to rewrite the whole thing, but rather shift the focus. Try rewriting the assignment in your own words to determine exactly what is expected of you. You may simply need to add a few sentences to your introduction and conclusion, or add a new paragraph that helps clarify your position. Don't stop reworking until your essay clearly and completely responds to the assignment.

Rewording Your Thesis

If your thesis isn't clear, or is not easily identifiable, you probably have one of these common problems:

- **No thesis.** Your essay may have a lot to say, but its paragraphs are not held together by one controlling idea. This type of essay is often the result of insufficient planning. If you took the time to consider your audience and purpose, brainstorm, and develop a tentative thesis and outline, you should be able to avoid this problem. Go back to your prewriting notes to find the main idea you started with, and begin drafting a thesis from there.

- **Your thesis isn't supported by your essay.** You do have a thesis, but the body of your essay supports another (perhaps similar) idea. This often happens when writers discover, through the drafting process, that they feel differently about their topic than they originally thought. As a result, they end up building a case for a different thesis. If your essay does indeed support an idea that's different from your thesis (and that idea still addresses the assignment), the easiest way to correct the problem is to rewrite your thesis to fit your essay.

- **More than one main idea.** If your essay has two, or even three, main ideas, you may not have sufficiently narrowed your thesis during the planning stage. Recall in Lesson 5 the discussion concerning the need to have a thesis that correlates with the *space confines* of an essay. It must be broad enough to warrant an essay-length discussion, and narrow enough to be able to complete a thorough discussion within those confines. Or, you may have discovered other interesting ideas while drafting and decided to include them. As a result, you have two or three underdeveloped mini essays rather than one fully developed idea. If you have more than one main idea, see if there is a way to tie them together. Otherwise, choose the better of the two and revise your essay to develop that idea alone.

Checking for Support

You'll also need to assess how well your draft supports your thesis, and how well your evidence, examples, and details support the ideas you put forth. Types of support include:

- specific examples
- facts
- reasons
- descriptions and anecdotes
- expert opinions and analysis
- quotations from the text

How Much Is Enough?

There is no hard and fast rule about how much support you need for an effective essay. But it's safe to say that one supporting idea is almost never enough. Two is better, but it may not be enough to make your claim. Three is often the magic number—it has "critical mass," and it shows readers why you think what you do. Four ideas are even better; beyond critical mass, they're a good solid amount of evidence.

Support That's Directly Related to the Thesis

As important as the amount of support is its relevance to the thesis. What good are ten supporting paragraphs if they're not supporting the right idea? Read the following essay carefully, paying particular attention to the support provided for the thesis.

When was the last time you told a lie? If you're like most people, it was probably recently. Did you know that you can also lie without even saying a word? This kind of lie can be even more devastating.

The poet Adrienne Rich said, "Lying is done with words and also with silence." To lie means "to tell something that is untrue." But it also means "to be deceptive." We often use silence to deceive. Rich is right. We lie with words, but also with silence.

For example, a man buys a necklace for his girlfriend from a thief. He knows the necklace is stolen and doesn't tell his girlfriend. As a result, she finds out it's a stolen necklace when she tries to take the necklace back to the store for repairs.

I'm guilty, too. I knew my friend's boyfriend was seeing someone else. But I kept quiet. I helped keep her in the dark. Then, when she found him out—and found out that I'd known about it—it was terrible. It destroyed their relationship and our friendship.

Looking closely at the two supporting examples, you can see that neither example addresses how these silent lies are more devastating than a spoken lie. Now the writer must make a decision. Should she expand each paragraph to explain how keeping silent was worse than lying aloud? Or should she revise her thesis to eliminate the idea that silent lies are "more devastating" than regular lies?

Choosing the latter, she revised her thesis once more and created the following thesis statement:

We lie with words, but also with silence. And these lies can be equally devastating.

Now the writer has two solid supporting examples for her thesis. But she should probably add as least one, and preferably two more, to strengthen her essay.

▶ Practice 1

So far, there are only two supporting paragraphs for the *lying with silence* draft. Add an additional supporting paragraph to strengthen and support this essay.

_____

_____

_____

_____

Strategies for Convincing

While this essay now has a clear, focused thesis supported by several examples, it still lacks persuasive power. Before you consider your check for support complete, consider whether you've applied the strategies for convincing discussed in Lesson 10. Ask the following questions:

- Are your supporting paragraphs specific?
- Do you have any unsupported statements?
- Have you established credibility?
- Do you acknowledge counterarguments?
- Do you make concessions?
- Do you avoid absolutes?
- Do you say anything that might offend your audience?

The examples in the *lying with silence* essay are not as specific as they could be. In fact, they would work better if they were expanded with more information that would show how people are affected by these silent lies. Instead of one paragraph for each example, two or even three would bring the examples to life and make them more specific. Because the essay relies almost entirely on examples for support, the more detailed those examples are, the more convincing they will be.

▶ Practice 2

On a separate sheet of paper or on your computer, revise one of the example paragraphs in the *lying with silence* essay to provide more information and specific details. Expand the example until you have two complete paragraphs.

▶ In Short

Revision deals with the content and style of the essay and should begin by addressing the big-picture issues: thesis and support. Look at your essay with fresh eyes, both literally in the form of trusted readers, and figuratively, as you reread after taking a break from your writing. Then, rework the essay to assure that it fulfills the assignment, contains a strong, clear thesis statement, and is supported with convincing examples and evidence.

Skill Building until Next Time

Use the read-aloud technique for another essay you're working on or that you wrote for another purpose. What did you notice about your writing? Do you like the way it sounds? Does it convey the meaning(s) you intended?

15 ▶ Revising Paragraphs

LESSON SUMMARY

This second lesson on the revision process shows you how to revise paragraphs for more effective organization and transitions. You'll also learn how to strengthen individual paragraphs.

T he next step in *re-visioning* looks at your essay with a stronger lens, examining it at the paragraph level. The first question to ask about paragraphs is also a "big picture" question:

1. Are you paragraphs in a logical and effective order?

Once you've addressed this question, you can look at each paragraph individually with the following questions in mind:

2. Does each paragraph have only one controlling idea?
3. Are there effective transitions between ideas?
4. Do special paragraphs fulfill their functions?

► Checking Your Organization

If your ideas don't flow logically, they'll be difficult for your reader to follow. Make sure those ideas are placed within the essay in order in which they make sense. Seven organizing principles were discussed in Lessons 6 and 7:

- chronology
- cause and effect
- spatial order
- analysis/classification
- order of importance
- comparison and contrast
- problem → solution

As you read your paragraphs checking for organization, consider the following questions:

1. **What organizing principle holds the essay together?** One overlying organizing principle should be clear. If you can't identify one, look carefully at how you presented your ideas. If you haven't used an organizing strategy, chances are your essay will feel disjointed to readers. Think about which strategy makes the most sense for your subject and purpose.

2. **Is this the most effective organization for your subject and purpose?** Once you've identified your organizing principle, consider whether it's the best one for your essay. For example, if you've used the block technique for a comparison and contrast essay, you might consider whether the point-by-point method would work better instead.

3. **Do any paragraphs or sections disrupt this organizational pattern?** If there is a break in your organizational structure, it should not only be intentional, but also serve a legitimate purpose. Perhaps you decided to keep the block comparison and contrast. In one section, though, you slip into the point-by-point mode and compare two items directly. Unless there is a solid reason for the inconsistency, such as making sure that those two items stand out as more significant than the others being compared, change that section to the block technique. Consistency makes your essay easier to read and understand.

▶ Practice 1

Substantial revisions have been made to the essay about "lying with silence." For each paragraph, note the idea and function in the space provided. The first two paragraphs are done for you. Then, answer the questions that follow.

PARAGRAPH	IDEA	FUNCTION
When was the last time you told a lie? If you're like most people, it was probably recently. In fact, it was probably more recently than you think. The poet Adrienne Rich said, "Lying is done with words and also with silence." We don't have to talk to tell a lie. Our silences can be just as deceiving—and just as devastating.	Lying is also done with silence and can be devastating.	Introduces the essay
You might be wondering how we can lie with silence. To lie means "to tell something that is untrue." But it also means "to be deceptive." There are many ways we deceive. Words are one way; silence is another.	Definition of lie	Explains how silence is also a lie
There's a difference between being silent because you don't want someone to know something and being silent because you want someone to think something that isn't true. The first is not a lie; it is not deceptive. The second, however, is a lie; the aim is to deceive. For example, imagine that I am in a job interview. If I don't tell you that I went to three different colleges, that's not a lie. But if I know you assume that I've graduated, and I don't tell you that I don't have a college degree, I am deliberately deceiving you with my silence. I am "telling" you a lie.		
These silent lies can have consequences. For example, a man who buys a stolen necklace for his girlfriend could lose her trust, which could be detrimental to the relationship. More importantly, he could also face criminal charges. In addition, even she could be in trouble for possession of a stolen necklace.		
This man has committed a crime with his silence. By remaining silent, he not only puts the woman in jeopardy for legal trouble, but he also can get in a lot of trouble himself.		

PARAGRAPH	IDEA	FUNCTION
I'm guilty of silent deceptions, too. Last year, I discovered that my friend's boyfriend was seeing someone else. I kept quiet about it because I didn't want to hurt my friend. A few weeks later, someone else told her about the two-timing—and I told her I knew about it. She felt deceived, not only by her boyfriend, but by me, too. And those deceptions ruined her relationship with her boyfriend and our friendship.		
Silent lies can also happen between strangers. Imagine you're at a diner. When the server hands you your check, you notice that she made a mistake, charging you $12.58 instead of $15.58. But you don't tell her. Instead, you pay the amount on the check, plus a tip based on that amount, and pocket the difference.		
These silent lies can cause as much harm as those told with words. They can even have devastating, serious consequences. That's why the law should not only prosecute people who lie on the stand, but also those who tell silent lies.		

Questions

1. What is the main organizing principle of the essay?

_____

2. Is this the best organizing strategy for the essay? Why or why not?

_____

3. What would you suggest the writer do to improve the organization?

_____

► Revising Individual Paragraphs

To check the paragraphs that make up your essay, you'll need to examine your writing with a stronger lens than the one you used to for "big-picture" issues. You will be determining whether each paragraph has just one main idea, whether there are adequate transitions between paragraphs, and if your introductory and concluding paragraphs fulfill their distinct purposes.

One Controlling Idea

A paragraph is a group of sentences about one idea. That idea should be stated in a topic sentence, which is typically the first or last line. Topic sentences not only guide your reader, but they also link the sentences in the paragraph together by stating the idea that they all relate to. If you can't locate a topic sentence, should the main idea be stated in one, instead of implied by your examples?

If there is a topic sentence, does each sentence relate to it? In the *lying with silence* essay, each paragraph contains only one main idea except for the sixth paragraph. Here, the writer describes the lie and its consequences in one paragraph. It would be more effective to dedicate another paragraph to the consequences. The revised paragraphing then looks like this (topic sentences are in bold):

__I'm guilty of silent deceptions, too.__ Last year, I discovered that my friend's boyfriend was seeing someone else. I kept quiet about it because I didn't want to hurt my friend. A few weeks, later, someone else told her about the two-timing— and I told her I knew about it.

She couldn't believe that I deceived her like that. She felt just as betrayed as if I'd lied to her face about it. Her boyfriend's deception ruined their relationship. __My deception destroyed our friendship.__

Relevance

If you've identified more than one idea in a paragraph, you should probably break it into two paragraphs. But before you move text, make sure each idea is clearly related to the thesis. If it's not, it needs to be reworked or deleted. (If you didn't catch it when you were revising the big picture, here's another chance.) Remember the importance of maintaining focus in your essay—unrelated paragraphs not only get you off track, but also often confuse readers as well.

Development

Once you've identified the controlling idea of each paragraph, check to see that each idea is sufficiently developed. Topic sentences, like thesis statements, make assertions about your subject. And those assertions need support. Look carefully at any paragraph that consists of only one or two sentences. Chances are, they're seriously underdeveloped. The only time you should have a one-sentence paragraph is when you intentionally decide to emphasize the idea in that sentence.

Transitions

Transitions are the words and phrases used to move from one idea to the next. They help your words flow smoothly and show readers how your ideas relate to each other. In shorter essays, a phrase is usually enough to transition from one paragraph to the next. In longer essays, a sentence or two may be required to guide your reader to the next idea.

ORGANIZING PRINCIPLE	TRANSITIONAL WORDS AND PHRASES		
order of importance	more importantly in addition first, second, third, etc.	above all first and foremost	moreover furthermore
chronological	then before while afterward first, second, third, etc.	next after as since	later during when until
spatial	beside around beyond under	next to above behind near	along below in front of
cause and effect	therefore so consequently	because since accordingly	as a result thus hence
comparison	likewise in the same way	similarly just as	like
contrast	on the other hand unlike rather although	however but instead	on the contrary yet whereas

In the *lying with silence* essay, notice how the writer uses transitions to move from one paragraph to another. The first sentence of the sixth paragraph, "I'm guilty of silent deceptions, too" connects the previous example (the man who bought a stolen necklace for his girlfriend) to the next example, the writer's own silent lie. Then, the beginning of the second sentence uses the transitional phrase *for example* to lead readers into the support for that paragraph. In addition, the phrase *a few weeks later* provides a transition in the middle of the paragraph, connecting the writer's decision to keep silent with her friend's discovery of the deception.

To demonstrate how important transitions are, here's the fourth paragraph of the essay with transitions removed and then repeated with transitions intact (and underlined):

These silent lies can have consequences. A man who buys a stolen necklace for his girlfriend could lose her trust, which could be detrimental to the relationship. He could also face criminal charges. Even she could be in trouble for possession of a stolen necklace.

These silent lies can have consequences. <u>For example</u>, a man who buys a stolen necklace for his girlfriend could lose her trust, which could be detrimental to the relationship. <u>More importantly</u>, he could also face criminal charges. <u>In addition</u>, even she could be in trouble for possession of a stolen necklace.

Introductions and Conclusions

Both of these paragraphs must fulfill specific duties within the essay. While you're revising, you'll need to look closely at them to make certain they function properly.

As you reread your introduction, ask:

- Does it provide the context needed to understand my thesis?
- Does it clearly state the main point of my essay?
- Does it set the tone for the essay?
- Does it grab my reader's interest?

Notice how the introduction to *lying with silence* accomplishes each of these four tasks. It provides context by quoting Adrienne Rich's claim about silent deceptions. It clearly states the thesis in the last two sentences. It also sets the tone by using words like *deceives* and *devastating*, which will be repeated in the essay. In addition, it grabs the audience's attention by beginning with a thought-provoking question.

As you reread your conclusion, ask:

- Does it restate my thesis in a new way?
- Does it offer a new understanding?
- Does it provide a sense of closure?
- Does it arouse my reader's emotions?

While the *lying with silence* essay does a good job with the introduction, its conclusion needs work. Notice how it simply restates the thesis instead of putting it in different words. It does offer a new understanding, but goes too far by introducing a contentious new issue instead of providing a sense of closure.

▶ Practice 2

On a separate sheet of paper or on your computer, revise the conclusion to the "lying with silence" essay.

▶ In Short

To revise on the paragraph level, first check for your overall organizing principle. How have you arranged your paragraphs? Is this the most effective organizing strategy for your essay? Then check individual paragraphs to make sure they have only one relevant and fully developed idea. Next, check for transitions both between and within paragraphs. Finally, check to see that your introduction and conclusion fulfill their important functions.

Skill Building until Next Time

Look again at the essay you read aloud at the end of Lesson 14. Identify the organizing principle, the topic sentences, and the transitions used throughout the essay.

16 ▶ Editing

LESSON SUMMARY

Editing takes a closer look at your writing, through a stronger lens that highlights words and sentences. Are your word choices clear and direct? Are there any repetitive or awkward sentences or phrases? When you edit, you can clean up and clear up words and sentences to make them better convey your intended meaning and easier to understand.

T o edit your essay effectively, you'll need to read each paragraph a number of times, paying careful attention to your sentences and the words that comprise them. While some students edit well on the computer, many others work better on a hard copy. Unlike revising, which entails the possible reworking of large parts of your essay, editing is a word-by-word and sentence-by-sentence task. Taking pen to paper may help you focus more closely on the pieces that make up your essay, rather than the work as a whole.

As you read the hard copy of your essay, pen in hand, ask yourself the following questions. Circle any problems as you encounter them. You might also want to make a quick note in the margin with an idea or two about how to improve the problem(s).

- Are unnecessary words and phrases cluttering up your sentences?
- Do you repeat yourself? Rework your point so that you say it well the first time, and remove any repetitious words and phrases.
- Are there any clichés, pretentious language, or confusing jargon?
- Do you use the active voice whenever possible?
- Do you avoid using ambiguous words and phrases?

- Are verb tenses consistent?
- Is the antecedent for every pronoun clear?
- Do you use precise adjectives and adverbs?
- Is your sentence structure varied? Sentences should not be the same length, nor should they be repetitive in any other way, such as all beginning with a noun, followed by a verb, followed by an object.

After you've read your essay a few times and highlighted any areas that need improving, focus on one problem at a time.

Be Concise

Why use ten words to get across a meaning that could be better said in five? Those ten words will definitely waste your reader's time and probably confuse the point you're trying to make. Many of the words and phrases that follow are both well known and, unfortunately, well used. They don't convey meaning, and are therefore unnecessary. The following are three of the worst offenders, with usage examples.

1. *Because of the fact that.* In most cases, just *because* will do.
   Because of the fact that he was late, he missed his flight.
   Because he was late, he missed his flight.

2. *That* and *which* phrases. Eliminate them by turning the idea in the *that* or *which* phrase into an adjective.
   These were directions that were well written.
   These directions were well written.

3. *That* by itself is a word that often clutters sentences unnecessarily, as in the following example:
   The newscaster said that there was a good chance that election turnout would be low and that it could
      result in a defeat for our candidate.
   The newscaster said there was a good chance election turnout would be low and could result in a defeat for
      our candidate.

Word Choices for Concise Writing

WORDY	REPLACE WITH
a lot of	*many* or *much*
all of a sudden	*suddenly*
along the lines of	*like, such as*
are able to	*can*
as a matter of fact	*in fact*, or Delete
as a person	Delete

Word Choices for Concise Writing (continued)

WORDY	REPLACE WITH
as a whole	Delete
as the case may be	Delete
at the present time	currently or now
both of these	both
by and large	Delete
by definition	Delete
due to the fact that	because
for all intents and purposes	Delete
has a tendency to	often or Delete
has the ability to	can
in order to	to
in the event that	if
in the near future	soon
is able to	can
it is clear that	Delete
last but not least	finally
on a daily basis	daily
on account of the fact that	because
particular	Delete
somewhere in the neighborhood of	about, around
take action	act
the fact that	that, or Delete
the majority of	most
the reason why	the reason or why
through the use of	through
with regard to	about or regarding
with the exception of	except for

Wordy and Concise Sentences

Wordy:	The students were given detention on account of the fact that they didn't show up for class.
Concise:	The students were given detention because they didn't show up for class.

Wordy:	Everyone who has the ability to donate time to a charity should do so.
Concise:	Everyone who can donate time to a charity should.

Wordy:	In a situation in which a replacement for the guidance counselor who is retiring is found, it is important that our student committee be notified.
Concise:	When a replacement for the retiring guidance counselor is found, our student committee must be notified.

Avoid Unnecessary Repetition

Unnecessary repetition is a sign of sloppy writing. It's easy to repeat the same thing, varying it slightly each time. It's harder to say something well once, and then write about your next idea or example. Repetition also wastes valuable time and space. If you are writing while the clock is ticking, or are limited to a number of words or pages, say it right the first time and move on.

For example:

Repetitive:	They met at 4 P.M. in the afternoon.
Concise:	They met at 4 P.M.

P.M. means in the afternoon, so there's no reason to say *in the afternoon*. It's a waste of words and the reader's time.

Repetition can be found even in short phrases. The list that follows contains dozens of such phrases that can clutter your essay. Most of them contain a specific word and its more general category. Why state both? The word *memories* can only refer to the past, so you don't need to say *past memories*. We know that blue is a color, so describing something as *blue in color* is repetitive and therefore unnecessary. In most cases, you can correct the redundant phrase by dropping the category and retaining the specific word.

Some of the phrases use a modifier that is unneeded, because the specific is implied in the general. For instance, the word *consensus* means general agreement. Therefore, modifying it with the word *general* is repetitive. Similarly, *mathematics* is a field of study, so it does not need to be modified with the word *field*. You can tighten up your writing, saying it well one time, by eliminating wordiness.

RETAIN ONLY THE FIRST WORD		DROP THE MODIFIER (FIRST WORD)	
any and all	**odd** in appearance	~~past~~ memories	~~terrible~~ tragedy
first and foremost	**mathematics** field	~~final~~ destination	~~end~~ result
refer back	**cheap** quality	~~general~~ consensus	~~final~~ outcome
close proximity	**honest** in character	~~various~~ differences	~~free~~ gift
large in size	**confused** state	~~each~~ individual	~~past~~ history
often times	**modern** in design	~~basic~~ fundamentals	~~totally~~ obvious
reason why	**unusual** in nature	~~true~~ facts	~~rarely~~ ever
heavy in weight	**extreme** in degree	~~important~~ essentials	~~unexpected~~ surprise
period in time	**strange** type	~~future~~ plans	~~sudden~~ crisis
round in shape			

Avoid Overly Informal and Overused Language

Words and phrases that are too formal, too obscure, or overused don't belong in your essay.

- **Vulgarisms**

  The last thing you want to do is turn off or offend your reader. Since it's difficult to know what kinds of language your audience may find offensive or in poor taste, err on the side of caution by not including any language considered even mildly obscene, gross, or otherwise offensive. This includes scatological and sexual terms, and words such as *butt* (as in "I worked my butt off"), *hell* (as in "hotter than hell"), *God* (as in "oh, God!"), and *damn*.

- **Clichés**

  Clichés should be avoided not only because they are too informal, but also because they are overused. Your writing must be in your own voice, without relying on stale phrases such as *one step at a time; no news is good news; have a nice day; when life gives you lemons, make lemonade;* and *no guts, no glory.*

- **Slang**

  Slang is nonstandard English. Its significance is typically far removed from either a word's denotative or connotative meaning, and is particular to certain groups (therefore, it excludes some readers who won't understand it). Examples include *blow off, canned, no sweat,* and *thumbs down (or up).* It is also inappropriate and offensive to use slang terms for racial or religious groups.

- **Buzzwords**

  Buzzwords are a type of slang. They're words (real or made up) that take the place of simpler, more direct words. They are, at best, pompous, and at worst, confusing. And, like other forms of slang, buzzwords don't belong in your essays. Examples include resultful *(gets results),* suboptimal *(not the best),* guesstimate *(estimate),* requisite *(necessary),* potentiality *(potential), and* facilitate *(help).*

Think Twice before Opening Your Thesaurus

Big words won't win points with your readers. Aim to sound like yourself, not to impress with your knowledge of ten-letter words. Here are three reasons to stop looking for and using so-called big words.

1. They sound pretentious (you're supposed to sound like *you*, not a politician or chairman of the board).
2. They can sound ridiculous (by using words that are not in your normal vocabulary, you run the risk of using them incorrectly).
3. They may appear as a "tactic" (your reader might think you are trying to add weight with words because you are worried your essay isn't well written or that your ideas aren't worth reading).

To the point: *I decided to keep it simple by packing only those things that I could carry in one suitcase.*
Thesaurized: I determined to eschew obfuscation by packing only those things that I could transport in one valise.

To the point: *At my summer job, I had the chance to learn about Information Technology as it relates to engineering.*
Thesaurized: At my summer employment, I had the fortuity to obtain IT-related information as it pertains to the engineering field.

- **Technobabble**
  Don't assume your audience shares your interests or familiarity with technology; write instead for a reader who has a broad knowledge base that is not expert in any subject. That means explaining anything your reader might not be familiar with, without talking down. Examples include *ISP* (Internet Service Provider), *screenagers* (teens who are online), *mouse potato* (technology's answer to the couch potato), and *I-way* (information superhighway).

Use the Active Voice

Verbs have two voices. In the **active voice**, the subject is the source of, or cause of, the action. In the **passive voice**, the subject is acted upon. In a personal essay, you are usually the subject. That means the active voice is much more effective in conveying your personality through your essay—you're the "actor," not the "acted upon." The active voice is also clearer and more direct. In the following examples, note the simplicity and directness of the first sentence in each pair. The second sentences, written in the passive voice, are clunky and noticeably longer.

Compare:
My friend asked for another helping.
Another helping was asked for by my friend.

I misplaced my wallet.
My wallet was misplaced by me.

The administration has selected three finalists for the open position.
Three finalists for the open position have been selected by the administration.

Avoid Ambiguity

Ambiguous means having two or more possible meanings. Ambiguous language can either be words and phrases that have more than one meaning, or word order that conveys a meaning different from the one intended by the writer:

The quarterback liked to tackle his problems.

This sentence can be read two ways: The quarterback likes to *deal with* his problems, or his problems are his opponents on the field whom he *grabs and knocks down*. This kind of confusion can happen whenever a word has more than one possible meaning. *The quarterback liked to address his problems* is a better sentence, and is unlikely to be misunderstood.

My advisor proofread my essay with the red sports car.

Here, the *word order* of the sentence, not an individual word, causes the confusion. Did the advisor proofread the essay with his car? Because the phrase *with the red sports car* is in the wrong place, the meaning of the sentence is unclear. Try instead: *My advisor with the red sports car proofread my essay.*

Clear Up Confusing Pronoun References

Pronouns (words such as *I*, *we*, *them*, and *her*) take the place of nouns. They should only be used when the noun to which they refer (known as the **antecedent**) is obvious and meaningful. Check the pronouns in your writing to be certain they are not one of the following:

- unclear
- too far from the antecedent
- useless

Correcting Ambiguous Language

Ambiguous: *When doing the laundry, the phone rang.*
Clear: The phone rang when *I* was doing the laundry.

Ambiguous: *She almost waited an hour for her friend.*
Clear: She waited almost an hour for her friend.

Ambiguous: *I told her I'd give her a ring tomorrow.*
Clear: I told her I'd call her tomorrow.

Ambiguous: *A speeding motorist hit a student who was jogging through the park in her blue sedan.*
Clear: A speeding motorist in a blue sedan hit a student who was jogging through the park.

More Examples of Pronoun Usage

Incorrect: Both Fellini and Bergman edited *his* movie.
Correct: Both Fellini and Bergman edited *Bergman's* movie.

Incorrect: Leave all ingredients out of the recipes *that do not belong* in a healthy diet.
Correct: Leave all ingredients *that do not belong* in a healthy diet out of the recipes.

Incorrect: *They* banned parking in their lot so the snowplows could do their job.
Correct: *The owners of the parking lot* banned parking in their lot so the snowplows could do their job.

Incorrect: The Civil War and the Spanish-American War took place in the nineteenth century. *It* was a turning point for the country.
Correct: The Civil War and the Spanish-American War took place in the nineteenth century. *The Civil War* was a turning point for the country.

Example: *Trini is interested in teaching and farming, which is her career choice.*

What is her career choice? *Which* could mean either teaching or farming, making it unclear. The writer needs to restate the career instead of using a pronoun in order to eliminate the possibility the reader will not understand the sentence. Corrected: *Trini is interested in teaching and farming, but farming is her career choice.*

Example: *They always talk about the dangers of global warming.*

This common pronoun error is known as an **expletive**: *They* is useless, because it appears to refer to no one. If the writer has that information, he or she can revise the sentence to be more precise: *The newspaper frequently has articles about the dangers of global warming.* If there is truly no *they,* the sentence should be revised by eliminating it: *There is much talk about the dangers of global warming.*

▶ Practice 1

Edit the following paragraph for clarity. Eliminate wordiness, unnecessary repetition, overly informal or overused language, the passive voice, and ambiguity.

I believe that the biggest and greatest challenge my generation will face will be ethical dilemmas created by scientific discoveries and advances. There has been a boatload of things discovered in this century, especially in the time period of the last few decades. Humankind is able to avail itself of a plethora of opportunities it heretofore was unable to take advantage of. But some very difficult ethical questions have been raised by these opportunities. They have given us new power over nature, but this power can easily be abused and misused.

Use Modifiers to Add Precision

Modifiers make your point clear while adding meaning and originality to your writing. Consider how powerful, specific adjectives and adverbs work in these sentences:

Sentence A: My grandmother put on her sweater.
Sentence B: My grandmother put on her *cashmere* sweater.

Sentence A: The football team practiced in the rain.
Sentence B: The football team practiced in the *torrential downpour*.

In both cases, sentence B allows you to hear the voice and impressions of the writer, giving a more accurate and interesting picture of the action.

The right modifiers (adjectives and adverbs) can also get your message across in fewer words. This is critical in an essay with a specified length. You don't want to sacrifice unique details, but sometimes, one word will do the job better than a few. For example, *Chihuahua* can take the place of *little dog*; *exhausted* can take the place of *really tired*; and *late* can take the place of *somewhat behind schedule*.

Vary Your Sentence Structure

The repetition of sentence patterns is not only boring, but in some cases, it can reduce your grade. The SAT essay, for example, is scored by readers trained to look for, and reward, variety in sentence structure. They can deduct a point or two for an essay filled with sentences that follow the same pattern. When you're editing your essay, check for monotonous sentence structure. Here's an example:

The plasma membrane is the outermost part of the cell. It isolates the cytoplasm. It regulates what comes in and out of the cytoplasm. It also allows interaction with other cells. The cytoplasm is the second layer of the cell. It contains water, salt, enzymes, and proteins. It also contains organelles like mitochondria.

Notice how each sentence begins with a noun or pronoun, followed by a verb. The rhythm created by this repetition is boring. A successful edit should vary the sentences:

The plasma membrane, the outermost part of the cell, isolates the cytoplasm. It regulates what comes in and out of the cell and allows interaction with other cells. The second layer, the cytoplasm, contains water, salt, enzymes, and proteins, as well as organelles like mitochondria.

The edited version combines sentences and uses introductory phrases and **appositives** (descriptive words and phrases set off by commas) to vary sentence structure. The result is a much more engaging paragraph.

▶ Practice 2

Edit the following paragraph, replacing general words with more exact ones and creating variety in sentence structure. (Note: You may also have to revise for clarity to address some of the problems in this paragraph.)

My generation will have many problems. One is the feeling of being overwhelmed by technology. Another is that the generation gap is growing. Another is that there are more people than every before. There isn't enough room for everybody. There are also limited resources.

▶ In Short

Wordiness and ambiguity often prevent ideas from coming across clearly. Edit your sentences to eliminate clutter and unnecessary repetition. Revise sentences that use overly informal or overused words, and exchange the passive voice for the active. Clarify ambiguous words and unclear pronoun references. Finally, improve your writing by using precise modifiers and adding variety to your sentence structure.

Skill Building until Next Time

Try writing some bad sentences. Use unnecessary words and repetition, jargon, pretentious words, unclear pronoun references, and ambiguous words. Avoid exact words and phrases, and repeat the same sentence structure. By trying to write poorly, you'll get a better sense of what to avoid in your writing.

17 ▶ Proofreading

LESSON SUMMARY

Before you submit your essay, there's one more important step: *proofreading*. Good proofreading involves far more than a simple run of spell and grammar check on your computer. In fact, those programs are not foolproof, and therefore, a reliance on them alone to find your errors is a mistake. However, they are not a bad place to start. This lesson explains how to use these tools to your advantage, as well as how to find and correct the most common grammar and mechanics errors.

Studies on grammar- and spell-check programs show that they are more effective when used as a first (not final) step in proofreading. After you've clicked your mouse through grammar and spell check, print out a hard copy of your essay and complete proofreading steps 2 and 3: Check for errors in grammar and mechanics.

▶ Limitations of Spell and Grammar Checkers

There is no excuse for not using spell- and grammar-check programs. They're fast and simple, and catch many common errors. However, they're not foolproof. Spell check has three important limitations you should be aware of:

1. **Non-Word versus Real-Word Errors**

   Most of us think of spelling errors in the first category—that is, a string of letters that does not make a real word. You might type *sevn* instead of *seven*, or *th* for *the*. Spell check is an excellent tool for catching these types of mistakes. However, if you are discussing the seven years of piano lessons you have taken, and you leave off the *s* in the word *seven*, the result is *even*, which spell check won't flag, because *even* is correctly spelled.

This is known as a real-word error. You have typed a legitimate, correctly spelled word; it's just not the word you meant to type, and it doesn't convey the meaning you intended. Spell check can't find these types of errors.

2. Proper Nouns

Spell check uses a dictionary that does not include most proper nouns and words in other categories, such as the names of chemicals. You can always add a word or words to the dictionary once you are sure of its spelling, but the first time, you will need to use another source (a reliable print one is best) to verify the spelling.

3. Errors Spelled Similarly to Other Real Words

If you misspell a word in such a way that it is now closer, letter by letter, to a word other than the one you intended, spell check will probably offer the wrong word as a correction. For example, if your essay includes a coffeehouse scenario, and you type the word *expresso*, spell check will correct the error with *express* rather than *espresso*. Similarly, *alot* will be corrected to *allot*. You must pay careful attention to spell check's suggested corrections to ensure the right selection.

Grammar-check programs are also effective but not foolproof. They can make two kinds of mistakes: missing errors, and flagging errors that are actually correct. The first problem, missing errors, is illustrated by the following examples. A grammar check on the following sentence did pick up the subject/verb agreement error (*I is*), but did not notice the participle error (*I studying*).

I is ready to take the exam after I studying my notes and the textbook.

Similarly, the punctuation problems in the following sentence were not flagged.

The recipe, calls for fifteen ingredients and, takes too long to prepare.

When grammar check does highlight an error, be aware that it may in fact be correct. But if your knowledge of grammar is limited, you will not know whether to accept grammar check's corrections. To further complicate matters, you may be offered more than one possible correction, and will be asked to choose between them. Unless you are familiar enough with the specific problem, this may be no more than a guess. It is important to understand the type of error highlighted, and get more information if you are not sure about it.

Professional Proofreading Tricks

1. **Take your time.** Studies show that waiting at least 20 minutes before proofreading your work can increase your likelihood of finding errors. Get up from your computer, take a break or move on to some other task, and then come back to your writing.
2. **Read backward.** Go through your writing from the last word to the first, focusing on each individual word, rather than on the context.
3. **Ask for help.** A pair of fresh eyes may find mistakes that you have overlooked dozens of times, and one or more of your colleagues or friends may be better at finding spelling and grammar errors than you are.
4. **Go under cover.** Print out a draft copy of your writing, and read it with a blank piece of paper over it, revealing just one sentence at a time. This technique will encourage a careful line-by-line edit.
5. **Watch the speed limit.** No matter which proofreading technique(s) you use, slow down. Reading at your normal speed will not give you enough time to spot errors.
6. **Know thyself.** Keep track of the kinds of errors you typically make. Common spelling errors can be caught by spell check if you add the word or words to the spell-check dictionary. When you know what you are looking for, you are more likely to find it.

▶ Proofreading for Grammar

Grammar refers to the hundreds of rules that govern sentences. Space confines limit this book's discussion of those rules to three of the most common errors:

- confusing words (*they're, there, their*)
- agreement (singular nouns with singular verbs, plural nouns with plural verbs)
- run-ons and sentence fragments

Confusing Words

Often, words are confused because the writer is in a hurry. It's not a matter of needing to learn the meaning of the words, but rather taking the time to check for accuracy. However, certain groups of words are commonly confused because not only do they sound or look alike, but also their meanings may be close enough to cause hesitation. Check the following list for those you're unsure of, and commit that shorter list to memory.

WORD	DEFINITION OR USAGE
accept (*verb*)	to recognize
except (*prep.*)	excluding
affect (*verb*)	to influence
effect (*noun*)	result
effect (*verb*)	to bring about
among (*prep.*)	to compare three or more people or things
between (*prep.*)	used for two people or things

WORD	DEFINITION OR USAGE
beside (*adj.*)	next to
besides (*adv.*)	in addition to
complement (*noun*)	match
compliment (*noun*, *verb*)	praise; to give praise
desert (*noun*)	arid, sandy region
dessert (*noun*)	sweet served after a meal
e.g.	abbrev. for Latin *exempli gratia* (*free example* or *for example*)
i.e.	abbrev. for Latin *id est* (*it is* or *that is*)
elicit (*verb*)	to stir up
illicit (*adj.*)	illegal
farther (*adv.*)	beyond
further (*adj.*)	additional
imply (*verb*)	to hint or suggest
infer (*verb*)	to assume, deduce
its (*pronoun*)	belonging to it
it's (*contraction*)	contraction of it is

Hint: Unlike most possessives, it doesn't have an apostrophe.

WORD	DEFINITION OR USAGE
lay (*verb*)	the action of placing or putting an item somewhere; a transitive verb, meaning something you do *to* something else
lie (*verb*)	to recline or be placed (a lack of action); an intransitive verb, meaning it does not act on anything or anyone else
loose (*adj.*)	not restrained, not fastened
lose (*verb*)	to fail to win; be deprived of
principal (*adj.*)	main
principal (*noun*)	person in charge
principle (*noun*)	standard
stationary (*adj.*)	not moving
stationery (*noun*)	writing paper
than (*conj.*, *prep.*)	in contrast to
then (*adv.*)	next

WORD	DEFINITION OR USAGE
that (*pronoun*)	introduces a restrictive (or essential) clause
which (*pronoun*)	introduces a nonrestrictive (or nonessential) clause

Hint: Imagine a parenthetical *by the way* following the word *which*. "The book, which (by the way) Joanne prefers, is her first novel," is incorrect. Therefore, it should read, "The book that Joanne prefers is her first novel." "Lou's pants, which (by the way) are black, are made of leather," is correct.

WORD	DEFINITION OR USAGE
their (*pronoun*)	belonging to them
there (*adv.*)	in a place
they're (*pronoun*)	contraction for they are
who (*pronoun*)	substitute for he, she or they
whom (*pronoun*)	substitute for him, her or them
your (*pronoun*)	belonging to you
you're (*pronoun*)	contraction for you are

▶ Agreement

Agreement refers to the balance of sentence elements such as subjects and verbs and pronouns and antecedents. (An **antecedent** is the noun a pronoun replaces.) To agree, singular subjects require singular verbs, and plural subjects require plural verbs. Likewise, singular nouns can be replaced only by singular pronouns, and plural nouns require plural pronouns.

Most of these errors are easy to spot. If you mistype "The scientists was working on an important experiment," you (or, possibly, your grammar-check program) will catch it. But problems arise when a phrase or phrases separate the subject and verb or noun and pronoun. Here's an example:

"Eat, drink, and be merry," is a label associated with Greek philosopher Epicurus, but like most catchy slogans, they simplify what is actually a rich and complex message.

Notice how the phrase *like most catchy slogans* can mislead you. If you assume *slogans* is the subject, then the pronoun *they* and the verb *simplify* seem correct—they agree with the plural subject. But look again at the sentence. *Slogans* isn't the subject of the verb *simplify*. What is simplifying? Not the *slogans*, but the *label* "Eat, Drink, and Be Merry"—a singular noun. Thus, the pronoun must be *it* and the verb must be *simplifies* to agree with the subject.

Run-ons and Sentence Fragments

Complete sentences require a noun and verb, and express a fully developed thought. Two common sentence errors are extremes. **Sentence fragments** stop too quickly; they are phrases that are not whole thoughts. **Run-on sentences** don't stop soon enough; they include two or more complete clauses or sentences.

Sentence fragments are often missing a subject or verb, and may be phrases or parts of other sentences. Be aware that fragments can sometimes be difficult to identify because even though they don't express complete thoughts, they can be long and appear correct. Here are a few examples, with corrections:

Because she had to stop studying and go to lacrosse practice.
Cried a lot.
When we finished the game after the sun began setting.

She had to stop studying and go to lacrosse practice.
Sheu Ling cried a lot.
We finished the game after the sun began setting.

Run-on sentences are made up of two or more independent clauses or complete sentences placed together into one sentence without proper punctuation. For example:

We were hungry and John was tired so we had to stop at the first rest area that we saw.
Kim studied hard for the test that's why he got an A.
Patty took flying lessons every Saturday so she couldn't go to the picnic and she couldn't go to the graduation party either *but she has already signed up for another group of flying lessons because she likes it so much.*

Here's how to fix run-on sentences:

1. Separate the clauses with a **period**. Example: *We are here. You are not.*
2. Connect the clauses with a **comma** *and* a **conjunction** (*and, or, nor, for, but, so, yet*). *We are here, but you are not.*
3. Connect the clauses with a **semicolon** (and possibly an adverb such as *however, therefore,* or *otherwise,* making sure it expresses the right relationship between the two ideas). *We are here; you are not.*

The previous run-ons can be corrected as follows:

We were hungry and John was tired, so we had to stop at the first rest area that we saw.
Kim studied hard for the test; that's why he got an A.
Patty took flying lessons every Saturday, so she couldn't go to the picnic. She couldn't go to the graduation party either, but she has already signed up for another group of flying lessons because she likes it so much.

▶ Practice 1

Proofread the following paragraph for grammatical mistakes. Make changes to improve the clarity and structure of the sentences as well.

Comic relief is important in tragedies, readers need a little relief from all of the sadness in the story. For example, Hamlet. Ophelia had just died. The next seen is with the gravedigger. Who is a very funny character. They dug up a skull and makes along speech about who the skull might have belonged to. Even though its about death. The scene is funny, it lets readers forget about the tragedy for a moment and laugh.

▶ Proofreading for Mechanics

Mechanics refers to the standard practices for the presentation of words and sentences, including capitalization, punctuation, and spelling. As with grammar, there are many rules for mechanics, but here we will cover the ones that cause essay writers the most problems. See the Appendix for more thorough grammar and mechanics resources.

Capitalization

Capitalization is necessary both for specific words and to start sentences and quotes. However, many writers overuse it. Only six occasions require capitalization:

1. the first word of a sentence
2. proper nouns (names of people, places, and things)
3. the first word of a complete quotation, but not a partial quotation
4. the first, last, and any other important words of a title
5. languages
6. the pronoun *I*, and any contractions made with it

Punctuation

There are dozens of punctuation marks in the English language. They're used to separate ideas, form words, and make the meanings of sentence clear. Poor punctuation can confuse your readers and change your intended meaning. For example, one comma completely changes the meaning of this short sentence:

Don't call me, stupid!
Don't call me stupid!

Here's a quick punctuation review:

IF YOUR PURPOSE IS TO	USE THIS PUNCTUATION	EXAMPLE
end a sentence	**period**[.]	Use a period to end a sentence.
connect complete sentences	**semicolon**[;] or a **comma** [,] *and* a **conjunction** [and, or, nor, for, so, but, yet]	A semicolon can connect two sentences; it is an excellent way to show that two ideas are related.
connect items in a list	**comma** [,] but if one or more items in that list already has a comma, use a **semicolon** [;]	The table was overturned, the mattress was torn apart, and the dresser drawers were strewn all over the floor. The castaways included a professor, who was the group's leader; an actress; and a housewife.
introduce a quotation or explanation	**colon** [:] or **comma** [,]	Colons have three functions: introducing long lists, introducing quotations, and introducing explanations. He said, "This simply won't do."
indicate a quotation	**quotation marks** [" "]	"To be or not to be?" is one of the most famous lines from *Hamlet*.
indicate a question	**question mark** [?]	Why are so many engineering students obsessed with *Star Trek*?
connect two words that work together	**hyphen** [-]	brother-in-law, well-known author
separate a word or phrase for emphasis	**dash** [—]	I never lie—never.
separate a word or phrase that is relevant but not essential information	**parenthesis** [( )]	There is an exception to every rule (including this one).
show possession or contraction	**apostrophe** [']	That's Jane's car.

Spelling

Proofreading for spelling errors after you've run a spell-check program means looking carefully for real-word errors. If you typed *tow* instead of *two,* that mistake is still in your essay, waiting for you to find it. Use the professional proofreading tricks on page 133 (especially numbers 2, 4, and 6) to scan for mistakes.

▶ Practice 2

Proofread the following paragraph for mechanical errors:

Compact discs (CDs), which may be found in over 25 million american homes not to mention backpacks and auto-mobiles first entered popular culture in the 1980's. But there history goes back to the 1960's, when an Inventor named James Russell decided to create and alternative to his scratched and warped phonograph records, a system that could record, store, and replay music without ever whereing out.

▶ In Short

Proofreading is the final step in the writing process. Begin by running spell- and grammar-check programs, being mindful of their shortcomings. Then, using the professional proofreaders' tips, study your essay for errors in grammar. In particular, look out for confused words, agreement mistakes, and run-on sentences and fragments. Finally, check your mechanics. Have you used capital letters and punctuation marks correctly? Are there real-word or other spelling errors that spell check missed?

Skill Building until Next Time

Get a good grammar handbook that includes practice exercises (see the Additional Resources for suggestions) and review the rules of grammar and mechanics. Do you remember the pretest at the beginning of the book? Note the areas that give you trouble. Work through the appropriate sections of the book to address your weak points. If you tend to write sentence fragments, for example, spend extra time working through the exercises on complete sentences.

Taking an
Essay Exam

THIS FOURTH AND final section deals with a specific essay-writing situation: the timed essay exam. You can use most of the writing strategies you've learned so far, but because your time is limited, this kind of essay requires a unique approach. The lessons in this section will give you specific strategies for tackling essay exams, from the crucial planning stage through the editing process.

18 ▶ Preparing for an Essay Exam

LESSON SUMMARY

Essay exams are stressful. You have to come up with a well-written piece under a strict time restraint in a room crowded with other students. How can you alleviate some of that stress and walk into the testing room with confidence? The answer is preparation.

Writing an essay in an exam situation, with the clock ticking, is very different from other types of essay writing. Of course, the fundamentals of good writing don't change (which is why Sections 1–3 apply to any type of essay). What changes is your approach. When you have just 25 minutes (SAT), 30 minutes (ACT), or an hour (many state tests, such as Regents'), you must use your time wisely. Every minute counts.

The way to take full advantage of every minute is to prepare; gather all available information about the test beforehand, checking the resources in the Additional Resources section of this book, as well as your exam's website. Understand the type of prompt you'll find on the test, know how to organize your thoughts, and be able to expand prewriting notes into paragraphs. Take timed practice exams not only to get used to the situation, but also to identify your strengths and weaknesses. When you take a timed essay exam, preparation can mean the difference between a great score and a poor one.

► Types of Exams

Spend time learning the general features of the essay you'll be taking. Understand the topics and what scorers will be looking for. Study the instructions for your essay carefully (they're all online)—think of how much time you'll save during the exam if you don't have to read them. Finally, visit the test website to get the most up-to-date information about topics and any changes made to the tests.

ACT

The ACT Plus Writing Test is optional. Some schools require the test, so check with those you plan on applying to before you make your decision to register for it. The essay is written in response to a prompt concerning an issue of relevance to high school students. You'll need to take a stand on that topic, support your point of view, and present a counterargument.

Here's a sample prompt:

In an effort to reduce juvenile violence and crime, many towns have chosen to enforce curfews on minors under the age of eighteen. These curfews make it illegal for any minor to loiter, wander, stroll, or play in public streets, highways, roads, alleys, parks, playgrounds, or other public places between the hours of 10:00 P.M. and 5:00 A.M. These curfews also make it illegal for parents or legal guardians to allow minors to congregate in certain public places unsupervised. Those who support these curfews believe they would reduce community problems such as violence, graffiti, and drugs, and would force parents and guardians to take responsibility for their children's whereabouts. Those who oppose curfews for minors claim these laws violate the Fourteenth Amendment rights of life and privilege for U.S. citizens. They also believe that such curfews stereotype minors by presupposing that citizens under the age of eighteen are the only people who commit crimes.

In your essay, take a position on this question. You may write about either one of the two points of view given, or you may present a different point of view on this topic. Use specific reasons and examples to support your position.

Two trained readers will score your essay on a scale of 1–6; the highest possible score is a 12, and the lowest is a 2. Those readers will evaluate how well you:

- supported your position
- maintained focus on the topic
- developed and organized your position logically
- supported your ideas
- adhered to the rules of standard written English

For the latest information about the test, check www.act.org.

GED

The General Educational Development test contains a 45-minute writing section in which test takers must develop an expository essay that includes personal observations, knowledge, and experience. The typical GED essay is about 250 words in length, written on your choice of five topics. A list of possible topics, as well as some test-taking hints, may be found at http://www.cdlponline.org/gedprint/files/GED10.pdf. The official GED Testing Service website offers links to your jurisdiction's testing program, which may differ slightly from that of other states. Check www.acenet.edu/clll/ged/index.cfm for the latest information.

Those who score the GED essay read between 25 and 40 essays an hour. They look for:

- well-focused main points
- clear organization
- development of ideas
- appropriate sentence structure and word choice
- correct punctuation, grammar, and spelling

SAT

With just 25 minutes to write, you won't be expected to turn in a final draft essay when taking the SAT. Minor errors in grammar, usage, and mechanics are not weighed against you. Scorers instead read the essay to get an overall impression of your writing ability. They look for evidence of critical thinking: how well you responded to the topic, developed a point of view, and used appropriate examples and evidence to support your position. Is your essay clearly focused, and does it transition smoothly from one point to the next? Do you show evidence of having a varied and intelligent vocabulary?

You'll get either a "response to a quote" or a "complete the statement" prompt. The former has one or two quotes on a topic—you'll need to take a stand on that topic in your essay. The latter asks you to fill in the blank in a sentence, and write an essay based on your completed sentence. The latest information on the SAT essay may be found at www.collegeboard.com.

Regents' and Other Exit Exams

More than 25 states, including California, Alaska, North Carolina, and Texas, require a passing grade on an exit exam to be eligible for high school graduation. These tests vary, so it is important to get specific information about the test you are preparing to take. However, most exit exams allow 60 minutes to develop an essay based on one of a choice of topics. A list of topics for Georgia's Regents' exam, for example, may be found at www.gsu.edu/~wwwrtp/topics.htm (but remember to check with your school regarding the test you will be given).

A typical exit essay is approximately 1,500 words. Possible topics include responses to literature, biographical narratives, and even business letters. Those who grade exit essay exams ask:

- How well did you address the topic?
- Were your ideas organized?
- Did you develop major points, and support them with details and examples?
- Were your word choices and sentence structure effective and varied?
- How consistent was your style (paragraphing), grammar, spelling, and punctuation?
- Did you express yourself freshly and uniquely?

▶ Types of Essays

You have been assigned dozens of essays during high school. They might have been a response to something you read, an argument about a particular topic, or an explanation of an event or other subject of study. In fact, there are countless types of essays. However, almost all timed essay exams fall into one of two major categories: expository or persuasive. In fact, the ACT and SAT call exclusively for persuasive essays.

Expository

An **expository** essay gives directions, instructions, or explanations. It informs by presenting the writer's knowledge about the topic to the reader. You might be asked to *define*, *compare* and/or *contrast*, or *explain* cause and effect. In fact, think of the verbs used in your topic as *key words* that clue you in to the fact that you are being asked to write an expository essay. These key words include:

- **Compare:** examine qualities or characteristics to note and discuss similarities and differences
- **Contrast:** examine two or more ideas, people, or things, stressing their differences
- **Define:** give a clear, authoritative meaning that identifies distinguishing characteristics
- **Describe:** relate the details that make the subject in question unique
- **Diagram:** create a graphic organizer that explains your answer
- **Discuss:** examine the subject(s) thoroughly, and give a detailed explanation of its strengths and weaknesses
- **Enumerate:** determine the points you must make, and present them in a list or outline form
- **Explain:** clarify meaning in a straightforward fashion, paying attention to the reasons for a situation
- **Illustrate:** use examples, graphic organizers, evidence, or analogies to give meaning or answer a problem
- **Interpret:** explain the meaning of something or solve a problem using personal opinions, judgments, or reactions
- **List:** see *enumerate*
- **Narrate:** explain an occurrence by describing it as a series of chronological events
- **Outline:** describe in an organized fashion, systematically, highlighting only the major points (details not necessary)
- **Relate:** explain the associations or connections between two or more things, events, circumstances, or even people; may also be used to mean *narrate* (see *narrate*)
- **Recount:** see *narrate*
- **Review:** critically examine the topic, event, idea, or thing in question, discussing major points and their strengths and/or weaknesses
- **State:** express major points concisely, without using examples or details
- **Summarize:** see *state*
- **Trace:** similar to narrate; describe the chronology of an event to reveal its meaning

The Best Way to Achieve a High Score

The scorers of every type of timed essay agree on one significant point: You must support your essay with details, examples, and evidence. Not only will they strengthen your argument, but they will make your writing come alive. Common advice for essay exam takers is to include at least one sentence in each paragraph that begins with the words *For example*. Compare these sentences:

High school seniors should be allowed open campuses, on which they can arrive in time for their first class, leave during free periods, and come back to school for their other classes. There is no reason to treat high school seniors like children by making them stay in school all day when they don't have classes to attend all day. Seniors can handle the extra responsibility.

High school seniors should be allowed open campuses, on which they can arrive in time for their first class, leave during free periods, and come back to school for their other classes. Seniors are given freedom and responsibility in many other areas of their lives; for example, the ability to drive a car. Seniors are also permitted to vote, and to prepare for their futures through the college admissions process or vocational training.

The first example uses generalizations and unsubstantiated claims ("no reason to treat [them] . . . ," "can handle the extra responsibility"), which weaken the argument. The second uses evidence, such as the responsibility of driving and voting, to make the case for open campuses. Remember to back up what you say with evidence, details, and other types of examples.

Persuasive

In a **persuasive**, or **argument**, essay, you choose one idea and show why it is more legitimate or worthy than another. Your purpose is not to merely show your side, but to convince your reader why your side is best. In order to convince effectively, you must base your argument on reasoning and logic. The most important strategy for the persuasive essay is to choose the side that has the best, or most, evidence. If you believe in that side, your argument will most likely be even stronger (although you don't have to believe in it to write a good essay).

An important component of a persuasive essay is the inclusion of other sides or points of view. In fact, the scoring rubric for the ACT essay notes specifically that readers will be looking for counterarguments. Counterarguments are presented in order to be refuted or weakened, thereby strengthening the case for your side. However, it is important to use reasoning and understanding to refute them. If you don't sound fair, or simply present emotional reasons why your side is best, you have weakened your argument. You must show that your idea is most legitimate in part because other ideas are weak or incorrect.

Key verbs that will help you identify a call to write a persuasive essay include:

- **Criticize:** express your judgment about the strengths and weaknesses of your topic, and draw conclusions
- **Evaluate:** assess the topic based on its strengths and weaknesses, drawing conclusions
- **Justify:** defend or uphold your position on the topic, using convincing evidence
- **Prove:** confirm or verify that something is real or true using evidence, examples, and sound reasoning

► Understanding Your Prompt

This advice might seem obvious, but it aims to correct one of the most common mistakes made on essay exams: Spend time understanding the type of prompt you'll encounter. Remember that your score depends in large part on how well you address that prompt (both the ACT and SAT essay directions note that an essay written off topic will be scored 0; a GED essay that fails to adequately address the prompt also gets the lowest score—a 1). Preparation materials, both in print and on the Internet, are available for every essay exam, so it's easy to familiarize yourself with them.

Many students fail to address the prompt because they didn't understand what it was asking them to write about. The best way to determine whether you understand it is to put the prompt in your own words, and then compare yours with the original. Are they nearly the same in meaning? If you have trouble with this exercise, try circling the verbs (key words) in the original prompt. These are the same key words you will look for during the exam. When you understand the key words, you can more easily write the type of essay required by the prompt.

► Budgeting Your Time

As you prepare to take your exam, familiarize yourself with its timing. Whether you have 25 minutes or an hour, you should complete three distinct tasks: planning, writing, and revising. The writing stage will take the longest, and, for essays that don't hold grammatical and spelling mistakes against you, the revising stage will be the shortest. But every essay should include all three.

Planning

Section 1 covered prewriting. Review in particular Lessons 3 and 4, and decide, based on a few practice essays, which brainstorming technique works best for you in a timed situation. Knowing exactly what you will do when you begin the exam will not only help you save time, but will also take some of the pressure off, too. Some exit exams (such as Indiana's Graduation Qualifying Exam) judge your prewriting notes, outlines, and other graphic organizers, making it even more important to choose a strategy that you know you do well ahead of time. Even if you are taking the SAT, and have just 25 minutes for your essay, spend the first 3–5 planning.

Your planning time, no matter which prewriting strategy you use, should involve the formation of a thesis statement and three or four main points. Any supporting evidence for, or examples of, those points should be included. Once you begin planning, don't be tempted to switch topics, which will waste valuable writing time. Allow a few minutes to think through the topic. You may cross off main points that don't work, or add a new one or two as you go.

Time Management

Set a schedule that allows for each step in the writing process:

- Spend the first $\frac{1}{4}$ of your time planning your essay.
- Spend $\frac{1}{2}$ of your time drafting your essay.
- Spend the last $\frac{1}{4}$ of your time editing and proofreading your essay.

► Practice

Set a timer for five minutes. Draft a thesis statement and create an outline for the following sample SAT essay prompt:

Some people say there are no more heroes, but I see plenty of heroic people all around me. One person I consider a hero is _____.
Fill in the blank in the sentence. Write an essay in which you explain your answer.

► In Short

The time you spend planning for and preparing to take an essay exam can mean the difference between a great score and a poor one. Do your homework by researching your exam: Understand how it's scored, what type of prompt(s) you'll encounter, what the directions say, and even how much space you'll be given to write in. Learn how to respond quickly to a prompt by practicing: Come up with a thesis statement and outline in just five minutes or less.

Skill Building until Next Time

Gather a couple of sample prompts online or from other books about your exam (see the Additional Resources section for a list of books and online resources). Set the timer for five minutes and practice writing thesis statements and outlines. The more you practice, the easier it will be to plan your essay on exam day.

19 ▶ Drafting, Editing, and Proofreading

LESSON SUMMARY

This lesson explains how to spend the other three-quarters of your essay exam time: drafting, editing, and proofreading your essay.

ou've studied your test and understand what it will look like (including the instructions), and how it will be scored. You've practiced drafting thesis statements and outlines from sample prompts. Now, it's time to write.

▶ Drafting

Because you're writing under a strict time restraint, essay scorers don't expect your essay to be perfect. However, they don't expect a sloppy first draft that needs plenty of revising, either. Think instead of creating a "polished rough draft," writing that's more refined than a typical rough draft, well organized, and with as few errors in grammar and mechanics as possible.

General Guidelines

- Use your outline as a guide. Don't go off on tangents, but adhere to your plan. If you come up with another strong major point, use it, but don't freewrite or ramble.
- Separate your major points into paragraphs; this organization will help your readers follow the logic of your argument.
- Avoid unnecessary words, phrases, and sentences. Don't repeat yourself or try to fill space with meaningless sentences such as "This is a very interesting question" or "Different people have different opinions on this subject."
- Keep your reader in mind. This person will give you a score based on how well you write and how well you addressed the topic. Don't risk alienating or offending this person by using a tone or words that are too formal or too casual.
- Write neatly. Your readers can't score what they can't read or understand. In fact, some exam readers may be unconsciously influenced by your penmanship. If two essays are of equal quality, and one is written neatly while the other is in a sloppy, rushed hand, the neater essay will probably receive a slightly higher score. Neat handwriting is more reader friendly, and it suggests that the writer has more control over the writing process.

▶ Editing and Proofreading

The revision step is not included in this lesson for an important reason. Revising takes too much time and involves too much shuffling of text to be accomplished in the time you're given to write your essay. Recall instead that essay exams should be "polished rough drafts." There won't be extra minutes to move sentences from one paragraph to another, delete chunks of information, or add many new points (and even if you did have the time, you'd create a mess that most readers wouldn't be able to make sense of). That's why it's critical to spend time developing an outline and to adhere to that plan once you begin drafting. An extra sentence or two inserted later to clarify a point is fine, but there isn't the space or time to allow for a real revision. Instead, focus on editing and proofreading your essay.

Hints for Taking the Exam

- Get a good night's sleep and eat a good meal before the exam.
- Bring all required items (such as writing instruments, identification, and/or a receipt).
- If there is a choice, read the prompts quickly to find the one you can think of the most examples and evidence for.
- Don't change your mind after making your prompt selection.
- Underline the key words in your prompt.
- Write legibly. You won't get points for neatness, but if they can't read it, they can't score it.
- Wear a watch, and make a plan for budgeting your time.

Some timed exams penalize for grammar, spelling, punctuation, and other errors in mechanics. All exams take off points for incomplete answers and failure to address the prompt. Leave some time to go over your work and correct or improve any errors. Be prepared to spend between 2–5 minutes editing and proofreading your essay. Check for the following:

In Paragraphs

1. details, examples, and supporting evidence in each paragraph
2. incomplete thoughts
3. rambling, off-topic thoughts
4. paragraph breaks that help the reader see your main points
5. effective transitions between ideas

In Words and Sentences

1. complete sentences (no fragments or run-ons)
2. variety in sentence structure
3. agreement
4. concise word choices
5. clichéd, pretentious language
6. ambiguity
7. passive voice
8. proper punctuation and capitalization
9. correct spelling

▶ Practice

Set aside 20 minutes for this exercise. Resist the urge to read ahead and think about the exercise before you're ready to complete it. When you're ready, set a timer and take the essay exam on the next page.

Stop!

Don't read the prompt until you're ready to write for 20 minutes.

"Ignorance is bliss." Write an essay in which you agree or disagree with this statement. Use an example from your personal experience, current events, history, literature, or another discipline to support your point of view. Use the following space to write your answer. You may use a scrap piece of paper to formulate ideas and take notes. Do not write on any other topic; do not skip lines.

_____

_____

_____

_____

_____

_____

_____

_____

_____

_____

_____

_____

_____

_____

_____

_____

_____

_____

_____

_____

_____

_____

▶ In Short

On an essay exam, you need to write a "polished rough draft." Follow your outline and write carefully but quickly. Make sure your thoughts are complete and your handwriting is neat. Don't repeat yourself, or use "filler" words and phrases. Choose words that concisely and clearly convey your ideas. Leave a few minutes to edit and proofread your essay, correcting any mistakes you might have made.

Skill Building until Next Time

Like all skills, your ability to write well under pressure will improve with practice. Chose one of the essay topics from the introduction of this book, set a timer for 30 minutes, and write another essay!

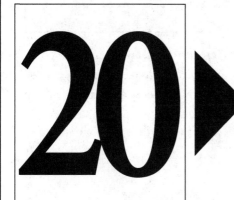

Sample Essay Exam Questions and Answers

LESSON SUMMARY

This final lesson presents two sample essay exam assignments and several sample responses. The responses are analyzed to give you a clearer sense of what constitutes a high- and a low-scoring essay.

When you're faced with any new task, it's helpful to see how others have performed it. That's why this final lesson is devoted to sample essay prompts and responses. There are two sample exams, based on the kinds of prompts used on the ACT, GED, Regents', and SAT exams. Five answers are given that cover a range of scores.

It's important to understand *why* each response received the score it did. You can study the scoring rubric for your exam either online or in a book, but you'll learn more by seeing what essays at each level look like. Our rubric (which may be found in the answer key) is based on those used to score the ACT, GED, Regents', and SAT essays.

► Sample Essay Exam #1

The photograph or picture that moved me the most is _____.

Assignment: Visual images have the power to inspire thought, evoke emotion, create mood, and even make political statements. Complete the statement and write an essay that explains your choice of image. You may choose any image, including a family photograph, famous work of art, drawing or painting done by a friend, or even a book illustration. Support your choice by using appropriate examples and details.

Time allowed: 25 minutes

Response #1

You might think a memorable picture would have vivid color, an appealing or inspirational theme, or be something you might want to display and look at every day. That is not the case with the picture that is most memorable to me. Rather, it is a large mural, painted in 1937 by the Spanish artist, Pablo Picasso, to protest the bombing of a small village in northern Spain.

Surprisingly, there is no vivid red color to show the flowing blood. One must imagine this, for the mural is startlingly gray, black, and white. But there is no avoiding the horror of the images. The figures are not realistically drawn, but are cubist and abstract, and it is apparent that innocent civilians are being slaughtered. A mother screams with her mouth wide open, her head tipped back in heart-rending anguish, as she holds her dead baby. A soldier lies dead on the ground, clutching his broken sword, and three other people are shown in shock and agony. Animals, including a tortured horse and a crying bird, are also portrayed as innocent victims of the massacre.

Some symbols are open to interpretation. What is the meaning of the bull, which seems simply to be observing, or of the light bulb emitting rays at the top of the mural? Does the bull symbolize brute force, and does the light bulb signify that there is hope? Yet there is no doubt that the distorted, horrible images are intended to shock the viewer. This depiction of human grief is a profound statement of the cruelty and senselessness of war. Limiting the picture to black and white adds a funereal element to the shocking depiction of the catastrophe.

The memory of the picture cannot be forgotten; it is a metaphor for the senselessness and the horror of war. While it was painted to protest atrocities in a long ago war, it is as relevant today as the recollection of the horrors of September 11. Perhaps it should be shown to all those who contemplate starting a war. Would it be worth it to have another Guernica?

Assessment

On a scale of 1–5, this essay received a score of 4. While the writing skills are effective, the organization could be improved. For example, the fact that the painting is black and white is mentioned in the second and third paragraphs, both times noting how the color choice adds to the mood of the painting. Paragraph 3 has a number of major points; it would be less confusing if each point had its own paragraph.

There is a clear point of view, and the writer has obviously studied not only the painting, but the language of art criticism as well. Examples are well chosen and numerous. Word choice is varied and sophisticated, and there are very few errors in grammar and mechanics. If the essay were better organized, and the writer had followed the five-paragraph form, it could have received a score of 5.

Response #2

The picture I remember is Guernica. It is by Picasso. It is not reelist. That means the shapes don't look real but you know what they are in real life. It is in black and white. It is not in color like most pictures. But it really gets to you. It shows people getting killed or who are already killed. The images make it so you won't forget it.

What this picture does is to make you know that war kills people and it is just awful. A baby is killed and a soldier is killed. A mother is screaming because her baby is dead. It kills people and it kills animals and even if you are not killed you will probly be screaming or crying. There are lots of ways that life gets destroyed by war. The painting shows many of them.

This picture could be for any war it doesn't matter. In that way it is a universal message. There is not anything in the picture that tells you where it is happening. You don't know who the people are. There are wars hapening today. People suffer now like in Guernica. You remeber it because it makes you upset and you wish there would never be a war. Then people wouldn't have to suffer. This picture is memrable because you remember how the people suffered and they probly didn't do anything.

Assessment

On a scale of 1–5, this essay received a 2. Organizationally, it has three paragraphs and each contains a main idea. However, two of them also include the introduction and conclusion. While they don't detract from or confuse the author's ideas, there are numerous errors in grammar and spelling. Most sentences are very short, and the lack of variety detracts from the essay. A strong point of view is maintained, but it gets lost in the unsophisticated and overly informal vocabulary.

▶ Sample Essay Exam #2

> An influential person is one who leaves a footprint in the sand of our soul. To me, the most influential person I can think of is _____.

Assignment: Complete the sentence above with an appropriate phrase. Then write an essay supporting your completed statement.

Time allowed: 45 minutes

Response #1

Have you ever imagined how your life would be different if a key person were not in it, like a mother, father, spouse, or child? Some people are so integral to making us who we are that without them, our very identity would be changed. My grandmother is a key figure in my life who has left an indelible impression on me. She is a woman of great influence because of her stability, her work ethic, and her independent spirit.

Grandma is the matriarch of our family. Because she has a close relationship with us and a great deal of wisdom, her seven children and 16 grandchildren often seek her out for advice. We look to her for advice on everything from how to potty-train a toddler to how to break up with a boyfriend. Grandma relishes the fact that we ask her for advice, but she never offers it without being sought out. She is like a rock: never changing. My own parents got divorced when I was 12, but I always knew that Grandma's house was a source of stability when the rest of my world seemed tumultuous. This sense of security has helped me face other challenges as they come along in life, like when we moved during my freshman year of high school.

Grandma also inspired me to pursue my goals. Because of the trials she faced without shrinking back, I am able to have the strength to work hard and try to realize my dreams. Grandma didn't have it easy. Because she was a single parent from a fairly young age, she had to work and sacrifice to support her children. She worked full time cleaning offices to save for her children's college educations. She received no help from the outside and was totally independent from her own family's help. Grandma always stressed the importance of education to all of us in achieving our goals. Grandma's example of hard work and her emphasis on education have strengthened me to pursue a college degree, and eventually a PhD. Even though I will have to work to get through school, I know that if Grandma worked while raising seven children alone, I can handle taking care of myself. Her tireless example is truly inspirational. She has also encouraged me in my chosen career, teaching, because she feels it will blend well with family life when I eventually have my own children.

Perhaps the most significant legacy Grandma has left me is her example of always voicing her opinion despite what others may think. Grandma would never bow down to prejudice; she never cared what people would say behind her back. In an age where segregation in social circles was common, Grandma's dinners after church on Sundays would look like a United Nations meeting. She would include all races and nationalities, and became close friends with a very diverse group of people. If someone tried to put down another race, she would quickly voice her disagreement. This refusal to be swayed by "popular" opinion had a huge impact on me, and is a guiding principle in my life today.

I certainly would not be the person I am today, inside or out, without the influence of my grandmother upon my life. I can only aspire to imitate her in her stability, her work ethic, and her refusal to be silenced by other people's disapproval.

Assessment

On a scale of 1–5, this essay received a 5. It shows an insightful understanding of the assignment. The writer chose a strong example of an influential person, and then skillfully developed her ideas with specific examples. We learn much about Grandma, and the writer constantly connects these details back to the main idea: that Grandma had a huge impact on her life in three major areas. The writer shows an excellent command of language. There are no grammatical errors, and she varies her sentence structure to make the reading interesting and enjoyable. This essay fully addresses all areas of the rubric in a strong way and is a good example of clear competence in writing.

Response #2

When someone comes into our lives for a long time, he or she leaves a footprint on our soul. I would say the biggest footprint in my soul comes from my little brother, Mario. Even though we've never had a conversation, Mario is a very big influence for three main reasons.

Mario is a peaceful person. He has a brain disease called lissencephaly. That happens when the brain is not bumpy and grooved like it's supposed to be. He has been like this from birth, and there's no cure. But Mario is like a little angel. He sits in his wheelchair and plays with his toys. Even though he is 8 years old, he can't walk or talk. But he has an inner peace that shines in his eyes. He never seems to worry about anything. He hardly ever cries or gets upset. He isn't impatient like the rest of us. He just takes each day, each hour, each minute as it comes. He has taught me about being peaceful no matter what is going on around me.

Mario has also taught me about unconditional love. Unconditional love means you love someone not because of what they can do for you, or what they have done for you, but just because you love them.

Mario also has influenced me to enjoy the simple gifts in life. I can run, walk, talk, and learn. Most of my friends complain about homework, girlfriends, and petty, stupid fights with their friends. But Mario, without saying anything, reminds me that it's all good. I have more than he does, and I should be content with what I have. I don't need to have the newest CD or my own car to be happy.

Not many people have a special gift like Mario in their life. I am really lucky because he has influenced me, I think, to be a better person. I've learned a lot about life from him, how to live and how not to live.

Assessment

On a scale of 1–5, this essay received a 3. The student shows a basic understanding of the assignment, using the example of his brother Mario to develop a response to the prompt. There is good development, particularly in the second paragraph, with specific examples. However, the second body paragraph, about unconditional love, is unsupported. Detracting from the essay are a very basic vocabulary and little sentence variety. This is a fair response with good ideas that would benefit from more sophisticated grammar and vocabulary and more concrete support.

Response #3

My mother is the person who influenced me the most. She is a very hard worker. She is a very devoted mother, and she is tough.

My mother works at Macy's, cleaning the rest rooms and straightening up the stock after the store closes. It is not an easy job, she does it from 12 midnight til 8 in the morning. My mother wanted to go to college, but her parents didn't have no money. She really want us to all go. I would love to make her proud of myself. That would be a great reward to her for all she did for us.

My mother cares about all the things that no other mothers pay no attention to anymore. She won't let me hang out with my friends without calling, no boys in the house when she's not home, I have to cook and clean, etc. She is a very devoted mother.

One day, some lady almost ran me over in front of my house. My mother went out there and tryd to find what the cause was. Well, the lady starting screaming at my mother, and she was the one at fault! My mother yelled back and even called the cops on this lady, she isn't afraid of anybody.

I think I will probably turn out to be just like my mother, and that would be fine with me.

Assessment

On a scale of 1–5, this essay received a 2. It shows a basic understanding of the assignment, but little development. The writer lays out three ways her mother has been influential in her life, but then fails to adequately develop them with examples. In the second body paragraph, the writer never makes a connection between her mother's strictness and being a devoted mother. In addition, she doesn't really discuss how this has affected her. There is a weak introduction with no real "hook," and a short conclusion that weakens the organization of the essay. The sentences are simple and contain noticeable errors, particularly run-on sentences. Overall, this response shows marginal competence in writing.

▶ Practice

Assess the essay you wrote for the practice exercise in Lesson 19. On a scale of 1–5, how would you rate your essay? What are its strengths? What are its weaknesses? Identify the things you did well in your essay. Then, list the ways you think your essay could be improved.

▶ Congratulations!

You've completed 20 lessons and have learned much about how to write essays that are more effective. To see just how much your skills have improved, turn the page and take the posttest. You should see a dramatic difference in your understanding of the writing process and in your ability to write clearly and effectively in an essay format.

To keep your skills sharp, write regularly. Start a journal or blog, write letters to friends, take a composition class, or join a writer's group. In addition, pay attention to what you read. Your writing will be positively influenced by good writing. See the Additional Resources section for suggestions.

Posttest

To gauge how much your essay-writing skills and your understanding of the writing process have improved, take the following posttest. Though the questions differ from those on the pretest, the format and material covered are the same, so you will be able to directly compare results.

When you complete the test, check your answers, and then compare your score with the one you received on the pretest. Your new score should be significantly higher, but if it's not, review the lessons that teach the skills on which you tested poorly. Whatever your score, keep this book on hand for reference as you continue on your academic journey.

You can use the space on the pages following Part 2 to record your answers and write your essay. Or, if you prefer, simply circle the answers directly for Part 1. Obviously, though, if this book doesn't belong to you, use separate sheets of lined paper to write your responses.

Take as much time as you need for Part 1 (although 20 minutes is an average completion time). When you're finished, check your answers against the answer key at the end of this book. Each answer tells you which lesson deals with the concept addressed in that question. Set aside another 30 minutes to complete Part 2.

1. (a) (b)
2. (a) (b) (c) (d)
3. (a) (b) (c) (d)
4. (a) (b) (c) (d)
5. (a) (b) (c) (d)
6. (a) (b)
7. (a) (b) (c) (d)

8. (a) (b) (c) (d)
9. (a) (b) (c) (d)
10. (a) (b) (c) (d)
11. (a) (b) (c) (d)
12. (a) (b) (c) (d)
13. (a) (b) (c) (d)
14. (a) (b) (c) (d)

15. (a) (b)
16. (a) (b) (c) (d)
17. (a) (b) (c) (d) (e)
18. (a) (b) (c) (d)
19. (a) (b) (c) (d)
20. (a) (b) (c) (d)

▶ Part 1

1. If your essay is well written, there's no need to completely fulfill the assignment.
   a. true
   b. false

2. In general, you should write for which audience?
   a. your classmates
   b. your teacher, admissions officer, or exam reader
   c. yourself
   d. a general reader

3. Which of the following introductory tasks does this introduction fail to do?
   In this essay, I would like to consider why the Great Depression occurred. Some people contend that it was caused by the stock market crash of 1929. Many economists point to the Smoot Hawley Tariff Act as the real reason. However, there is strong evidence to suggest that neither of these factors caused the Great Depression.
   a. Provide context.
   b. State the thesis.
   c. Grab the reader's attention.
   d. Set the tone for the essay.

4. In the following paragraph, which is the topic sentence?
   Too much sun can produce many negative consequences. First, it can dry your skin, which in turn reduces its elasticity and speeds the aging process. Second, too much sun can burn unprotected skin and cause permanent discoloration and damage to the dermis. Most importantly, long-term exposure of unprotected skin can result in skin cancer.
   a. the first sentence
   b. the second sentence
   c. the third sentence
   d. the fourth sentence

5. Which two organizational strategies does the paragraph in question 4 use?
   a. order of importance and comparison/contrast
   b. cause/effect and chronology
   c. classification and chronology
   d. order of importance and cause/effect

6. Three supporting ideas should be sufficient for any essay assignment.
   a. true
   b. false

7. A single-sentence paragraph is appropriate if
   a. you don't have any support for the assertion in that sentence.
   b. you have too many long paragraphs throughout the essay.
   c. it's a particularly well-written sentence.
   d. you want to emphasize the idea in that sentence.

8. Read the following essay assignment carefully. Which of the sentences best describes the kind of essay that you should write?
   In Civilization and Its Discontents, *Freud explains why he believes civilized people are unhappy. Summarize his theory and evaluate it.*
   a. Describe the main points of Freud's theory and assess the validity of that theory.
   b. Define "civilization" and show examples of civilized communities.
   c. Describe several examples that illustrate Freud's theory.
   d. Describe the main points of Freud's theory and express your opinion about his theory.

9. When revising an essay, which of the following issues should you address first?
   a. grammar and spelling
   b. organization and transitions
   c. thesis and support
   d. introductory paragraph

10. Which of the following sentences has the most effective word choice?
   a. She was scared.
   b. She was petrified.
   c. She was frightened.
   d. She was scared stiff.

11. Which of the following would be a problem in a concluding paragraph?
   a. It doesn't restate the thesis.
   b. It frames the essay.
   c. It arouses the reader's emotions.
   d. It doesn't bring up any ideas that aren't related to the thesis.

12. Which of the following is typically the best organizational strategy in an argument?
   a. order of importance (least to most important)
   b. order of importance (most to least important)
   c. cause and effect
   d. comparison and contrast

13. Identify the grammatical problem in the following sentence.

After he mastered the trumpet, he learned the guitar, and then learned how to play the piano, he went on to become one of the greatest jazz pianists in the world.

   a. sentence fragment

   b. agreement

   c. run-on sentence

   d. incorrect word choice

14. On an essay exam, most of your time should be spent

   a. planning.

   b. drafting.

   c. proofreading.

   d. editing.

15. An introduction should never be more than one paragraph long.

   a. true

   b. false

16. What is the main problem with the following sentence?

After his fight with Alan, he swore he would never let anyone use his car again without his permission.

   a. It's a run-on sentence.

   b. It's not properly punctuated.

   c. It's unnecessarily wordy.

   d. Its pronouns may be confusing.

17. A thesis should be which of the following?

   a. short

   b. clear

   c. assertive

   d. both **a** and **b**

   e. both **b** and **c**

18. Outlining should typically occur

   a. before you brainstorm.

   b. after you brainstorm.

   c. after you write your first rough draft.

   d. before you revise.

19. Which of the underlined words in the following paragraph are transitions?

Too much (1) *sun can produce many negative consequences.* <u>First</u> *(2), it can dry your skin, which in turn reduces its elasticity* <u>and</u> *(3) speeds the aging process.* <u>Second</u> *(4), too much sun can burn unprotected skin and cause permanent discoloration and damage* <u>to the dermis</u> *(5).* <u>Most importantly</u> *(6), long-term exposure of unprotected skin* <u>can result in</u> *(7) skin cancer.*

   a. 1, 2, and 3
   b. 2, 4, and 5
   c. 2, 6, and 7
   d. 2, 4, and 6

20. Credibility is best established by which of the following?

   a. expertise and freedom from bias
   b. expertise and education
   c. education and bias
   d. reputation and freedom from bias

▶ Part 2

Set a timer for 30 minutes. When you're ready to begin, read the essay assignment that follows carefully. Use the space provided to write your essay. Stop writing when 20 minutes have elapsed, even if you haven't completed your essay. When you're finished, look at the scoring chart in the answer key to estimate your essay's score.

Essay Assignment

Many people feel that a movie isn't a success if it doesn't force viewers to think about an important issue or idea. Others argue that movies are successful as long as they entertain us; they don't have to have any ideological, political, or social agenda. What do you think? Is being entertaining enough? Or should movies do more? Why? Provide specific examples to support your position.

Answer Key ▶

This section provides answers, sample answers, and explanations for the pretest, practice exercises, and posttest. Use the answers and explanations to assess your understanding of the lessons. But keep in mind that many of the exercises call for a written response, and those responses will be different for each person who completes the exercises. Suggested answers will demonstrate how one student successfully completed the assignment.

▶ Pretest, Part 1

If you miss any of the answers, you can find help for that question type in the lesson(s) shown to the right of the answer.

QUESTION	ANSWER	LESSON
1.	b.	11
2.	c.	8, 12
3.	d.	12
4.	a.	1
5.	a.	16
6.	d.	6, 7
7.	b.	2
8.	c.	6

QUESTION	ANSWER	LESSON
9.	b.	5, 8
10.	b.	9
11.	c.	10
12.	a.	13
13.	d.	15
14.	c.	18
15.	a.	3, 4
16.	b.	14–17
17.	e.	10
18.	b.	9, 15
19.	c.	16
20.	d.	11

▶ Pretest, Part 2

Use the following scoring chart to evaluate your essay. First, score your essay yourself (don't worry if some of the requirements are unfamiliar—a highly accurate score is not as important as the practice you received in writing a timed essay). Then, ask someone else (an English teacher or a friend with strong writing skills is ideal) to score it. After you assign a number for each of the categories shown on the chart, average the numbers to get an overall score.

CHARACTERISTIC	5	4	3	2	1
Response to Assignment	Completely fulfills the assignment; may go beyond the requirements to a new level.	Fulfills all of the requirements of the assignment.	Fulfills most of the requirements of the assignment.	Fails to fulfill a major part of the assignment.	Does not fulfill the assignment.
Thesis	Is clear, assertive, and original.	Is clear and assertive.	Is suggested but may be weak or unclear.	Is weak and/or unclear.	No recognizable thesis.

CHARACTERISTIC	5	4	3	2	1
Development	Several strong supporting ideas are offered; each idea is thoroughly developed.	Several supporting ideas are offered; most are adequately developed, but one or two are underdeveloped.	Offers some supporting ideas but not enough to make a strong case; ideas may be underdeveloped.	Few supporting ideas are offered; the ideas that are provided are insufficiently developed.	Little or no support is offered; ideas are poorly developed.
Focus	All ideas are directly and clearly related to the thesis.	Most ideas are directly and clearly related to the thesis.	A majority of ideas are related, but there are some loose connections and/or digressions.	Some focus, but many ideas are unrelated.	No focus; most ideas are unrelated to the thesis or topic.
Argumentation	Addresses counterarguments, makes concessions, and establishes credibility.	Addresses most counterarguments, establishes credibility for most sources; may neglect to make concessions.	Addresses some counterarguments but may neglect some major counterpoints; establishes credibility for some sources.	Fails to address most counterarguments; does not establish credibility for most sources; does not make concessions.	Does not address counterarguments, establish credibility, or make concessions.
Organization	Ideas are well organized; structure is clear; provides strong transitions throughout.	Ideas are well organized; good transitions throughout most of essay.	Essay has organizing principle, but pattern may be disrupted; some ideas are out of order; some transitions may be weak or missing.	Organizing principle may be unclear; many transitions are missing.	No organizing principle; weak or missing transitions throughout the essay.
Sentences	Ideas come across clearly; variety in sentence structure.	Most ideas are clear; may occasionally be wordy.	Sentences may be cluttered with unnecessary words or repetition; ambiguity may interfere with clarity.	Sentences are often wordy or ambiguous, interfering with clarity.	A majority of sentences are wordy or ambiguous, often interfering with clarity.
Word Choice	Precise and careful word choice; avoids jargon and pretentious language.	Most words are exact and appropriate; an occasionally ineffective word choice.	Mix of general and specific words; some pretentious language or jargon.	Mostly general inexact words; word choice sometimes inappropriate.	Word choice often ineffective or inappropriate.
Grammar	Virtually error free.	A few grammatical errors, but none that interfere with clarity.	Several grammatical errors; may interfere with clarity.	Many grammatical errors; often interfere with clarity.	Most sentences have grammatical errors, often interfering with clarity.
Mechanics	Virtually error free.	A few mechanical errors, but none that interfere with clarity.	Several mechanical errors; some may interfere with clarity.	Many mechanical errors that interfere with clarity.	Most sentences have mechanical errors that interfere with clarity.

► Lesson 1

Practice 1

1. Answers should mention a testing situation in which the scorers are not known to the test taker. There should be an explanation of the need to understand the test, especially its scoring rubric, in order to satisfy the requirements of the test.

2. a. In this case, you have been given a specific audience for whom to write: a Martian. However, a person (teacher, evaluator, or scorer) will also read your essay. Keep both audiences in mind as you write.

    b. The fact that your audience is a Martian, coupled with his question, can lead to an assumption that he has little knowledge of America. He may not have any knowledge of the concept of democracy, for example, or of freedom of speech. In fact, he may not even understand the words *country* or *nation*. For this assignment, you will have to explain yourself carefully, assuming no prior knowledge from your audience.

Practice 2

Answers must include a verb that specifies the goal. For example:

My goal is to explain the conflict that Hughes felt and show how he resolved his conflict.

► Lesson 2

Practice 1

1.

SUBJECT	DIRECTIONS
change in citizen's attitudes toward federal government in last decade	describe
what I think caused this change	explain
impact of this attitude on power of government	assess

2.

SUBJECT	DIRECTIONS
whether Celie has control over her destiny	answer and explain

3.

SUBJECT	DIRECTIONS
current definition of a planet	describe
differences between that definition and definitions of star and asteroid	contrast
how will current solar system change if size is a deterring factor in planet status	explain

Practice 2

Answers should be similar to the following:

1. Tell what citizens' attitudes toward the federal government used to be and what they are now. Tell what I think caused the change and why, and explain how I think this attitude has affected the power of the federal government.
2. Tell whether I think Celie has control over her future and why, using specific examples from the novel to support my answer.
3. Tell readers what the current definition of a planet is, and how it differs from the definitions of stars and asteroids. Explain how the solar system as we know it today will change if size becomes a defining characteristic of a planet.

► Lesson 3

Practice 1

Answers will vary. Here's one possibility:

When I was in the ninth grade, it was chemistry class, the first exam, and a lot of people were cheating. They all had cheat sheets and were even passing them back and forth. I was new, and I made some friends but wasn't really close to anyone, and I studied hard for the exam. I was really angry. The teacher looked up once or twice but didn't see anything. I was having trouble with one of the problems and thought about cheating, too. But I didn't have a cheat sheet. I knew if I told on the cheaters, it would mean trouble—didn't want to be an outcast. After the test, I typed a note and put it on the teacher's desk. Ms. Waller confronted us the next day—tensions were high! Cheaters were looking around trying to figure out who told—being new was lucky because no one suspected me—they blamed Pearl. Got really mean. I felt guilty. I confessed to Rob. But he ended up telling. Next day was one of the worst in my life. Someone threw food at me in the cafeteria, and everyone started calling me "rat," and worse. That name has stuck with me for two years, and it hasn't been easy making friends. I don't know if I'd do the same thing again. It's so hard to know what is the right thing to do, and how to fit in at the same time.

Practice 2

Here's an example:

A strong determining factor for my sense of identity is being a Vietnamese American.

- one language for home and neighborhood, another for school
- can't always express myself with American friends
- my parents get mad when I forget how to say something in Vietnamese
- having to serve as translator for my parents
- my accent
- how hard it was to learn to read English

- shyness, esp. in classroom
- people assuming I don't speak English
- stereotypes—I don't always eat rice!
- feeling most comfortable with other Vietnamese Americans

▶ Lesson 4

Practice 1

Answers should include all five questions (*who, what, where, when,* and *why*). Following are sample responses.

What are the benefits of school uniforms?

Who would decide what the students would wear?

Who would pay for the uniforms?

What about families who can't afford uniforms?

Why should the government make a decision about school children's clothing?

What effect would the cost of uniforms have on clothing budgets? (might save money)

Who would enforce the policy?

What about accessories, like jewelry or belts? Would they be regulated?

What about a sense of community? Would it be strengthened by uniforms?

Who might be upset or angry about uniforms?

Where are school uniforms required by public schools?

When would uniforms have to be worn? After school activities? School trips?

Practice 2

There are many ways to create a map for this assignment. Please see the example on page 40 in Lesson 4.

▶ Lesson 5

Practice 1

Responses will vary. Here is a possibility:

Assignment:	Identify a factor that you believe figures strongly in a child's personality development. Explain how that factor may influence the child.
Broad topic:	Factors influencing a child's personality development
Narrowed topic:	Parents
Sufficiently narrowed topic:	Parents who work outside the home
Further narrowed topic:	What kind of childcare parents choose for their children

Topic turned into a question:	How does the kind of childcare working parents choose affect a child's personality development?
Tentative thesis:	The kind of childcare working parents choose has a powerful impact on a child's personality development.

Practice 2

A successful response might look like this:

Assignment:	Discuss how sports influence popular culture. Use specific examples from the sports world.
Broad topic:	How sports influence popular culture
Narrowed topic:	How sports influence trends in fashion
Sufficiently narrowed topic:	How sports influence fashion and how sports heroes contribute to the rise of a highly profitable sneaker industry
Topic turned into a question:	How have certain sports figures helped popularize their sport and in turn influence fashion trends in sneakers among their fans?
Tentative thesis:	Charismatic sports figures can popularize their sport, widening their fan base, and in turn endorse products such as a particular sneaker that becomes a must-have trend in popular culture.

► Lesson 6

Practice 1

Here is a sample chronological outline for the freewriting exercise in Lesson 3.

1. Studied all week to get ready for exam.
2. Taking exam—seeing everyone cheating. Very angry.
3. Typing up note at home.
4. Leaving note on teacher's desk.
5. Teacher confronting class.
6. People deciding it was Pearl who told on them.
7. Begin mean to Pearl.
9. Feeling guilty.
10. Telling Rob.
11. Walking into cafeteria and having people make fun of me.
12. People avoiding me for weeks.

Practice 2

Here's an outline for the same freewriting exercise using cause and effect as the main organizing principle.

How I came to be called "The Rat":

1. Start with walking into the cafeteria and people pointing at me, saying, "Look, there's the Rat."
2. Describe how I'd left an anonymous note for the teacher.
   - describe why—the test
3. Explain how Pearl was blamed.
4. Describe dilemma—wanting to take blame off Pearl but not wanting to be hated by others.
5. Talk about consequences of doing what I thought was right:
   - nickname
   - people avoiding me
6. Describe how I feel about it now
   - still think I did the right thing, but should have given my name from the beginning
   - my fear of being outcast made me give anonymous note; that way the teacher couldn't help Pearl, or me, until it was too late.
   - learned that if I think something is right (or wrong), I should stand up for it (or against it) totally, not just halfway.

▶ Lesson 7

Practice 1

Here's an outline using order of importance for the school uniforms issue:

School uniforms: a good idea

1. Students and parents will save time and money.
   - spend less time worrying about what to wear
   - spend less time shopping
   - spend less money on clothes (fewer clothes needed)
2. Students will be more confident.
   - will equalize students who can afford the most stylish, expensive clothes with those who can't
   - will take the focus away from appearance so students can focus more on schoolwork
     - with more focus on work, students will do better in school
   - will help students feel like they belong
     - students need to feel like they belong to feel good about themselves
     - uniforms create a sense of community and belonging
3. Students will be better disciplined.
   - uniforms create a tone of seriousness
   - uniforms make it easier to focus on schoolwork

Practice 2

Part of an outline using comparison and contrast for the childcare issue might look like this:

Two options: nanny or daycare

1. One caregiver vs. many
    a. with nanny, child has one primary caregiver
        i. develops strong bond with one person
        ii. develops feeling of trust and security
    b. with daycare, child has several caregivers
        i. more difficult to develop strong bond with one person
2. One child vs. many
    a. with nanny, child gets great deal of individual attention (even if there are siblings)
        i. all of child's needs are attended to
    b. with daycare, child competes for attention with other children
        i. some of child's needs may not be attended to (at least not immediately)
        ii. child will develop social skills more rapidly by being in company of other children

▶ Lesson 8

Practice 1

Here's a possible response:

I never spend much time planning an essay. A lot of times I procrastinate and wait until the day before the paper is due to get started—especially if I don't like the assignment. Then I'll just sit down and write a draft. Sometimes I get stuck for a long time on the introduction. I have to have my introduction done before I write the body of an essay. Sometimes I get stuck too because I have trouble organizing my ideas. I usually don't outline unless my teacher says I have to. I should start doing outlines (at least rough ones) and start working on my essays earlier. I also need to make sure I am clearer about my audience and purpose. I think I'd write better (and be more relaxed) if I did some brainstorming as soon as I got the assignment, then drafted a thesis and outline, and <u>then</u> wrote a draft.

Practice 2

Here are some successful responses:

1. Briarwood offers everything I'm looking for in a college: a renowned child psychology department; a small, beautiful campus not too far from home; and opportunities to develop my leadership skills through extracurricular programs.
2. The use of DNA evidence in the appeals of death penalty convictions has changed the nature of the controversy surrounding this important issue.
3. My fascination with American history began when I read <u>The Grapes of Wrath</u>.
4. The Internet must remain a completely uncensored environment.

▶ Lesson 9

Practice 1

The following is the most logical way to divide the text into paragraphs (although minor variations are acceptable). Notice that each of the three parts of the personality gets its own paragraph. The topic sentence in each of those paragraphs (underlined) describes the main characteristic of that part of the personality.

Sigmund Freud, the father of psychoanalysis, made many contributions to the science of psychology. One of his greatest contributions was his theory of the personality. <u>According to Freud, the human personality is made up of three parts: the id, the ego, and the superego.</u>

<u>The id is the part of the personality that exists only in the subconscious.</u> According to Freud, the id has no direct contact with the reality. It is the innermost core of our personality and operates according to the pleasure principle. That is, it seeks immediate gratification for its desires, regardless of external realities or consequences. It is not even aware that external realities or consequences exist.

<u>The ego develops from the id and is the part of the personality in contact with the real world.</u> The ego is conscious and therefore aims to satisfy the subconscious desire of the id as best it can without the individual's environment. When it can't satisfy those desires, it tried to control or suppress the id. The ego functions according to the reality principle.

The superego is the third and final part of the personality to develop. <u>This part of the personality contains our moral values and ideals, our notion of what's right and wrong.</u> The superego gives us the "rules" that help the ego control the id. For example, a child wants a toy that belongs to another child (id). He checks his environment to see if it's possible to take that toy (ego). He can, and does. But then he remembers that it's wrong to take something that belongs to someone else (superego) and returns the toy.

Practice 2

Answers will vary. Topic sentences are in boldface.

1. **The demand for childcare workers is on the rise.** The government's Bureau of Labor Statistics (BLS) reports that employment in child daycare services will grow over 300% in the next decade. In 2002, about 750,000 people worked in child daycare services. By 2012, that number is expected to be about 1,050,000—an increase of more than 300,000 jobs.

2. When I was in kindergarten, I wanted to be an astronaut. When I was in junior high school, I wanted to be a doctor. When I was in high school, I wanted to be a teacher. Today, I'm 35 and I'm a firefighter. **I'm none of the things I thought I wanted to be—and I couldn't be happier.**

3. **While the proposed tax referendum sounds good, it's actually bad news for most citizens of Algonquin county.** It will not reduce taxes for middle-income families. In fact, middle-income families with children will pay 10% more per year, and families without children will pay 20% more. Further, the referendum actually decreases taxes for the wealthiest tax bracket. In fact, taxpayers in the highest income bracket will pay 10% less per year if the referendum is passed.

► Lesson 10

Practice 1 and 2

Look again at the outline for school uniforms (a response for Practice 1 of Lesson 7), noticing how each of the three main supporting ideas has several supporting ideas of its own. In the following, you'll find additional support for one of those ideas. Notice the mix of specific examples, facts, reasons, descriptions, and expert opinion.

- Students will be more confident.
  - will equalize students who can afford the most stylish, expensive clothes with those who can't
  - students often judge each other based on dress
- the most popular kids are usually the ones who can also keep up with the most recent fashion trends. "In any school yard, all you have to do is look around to see how important clothing is in defining groups and determining social status. The most popular students are always the ones in the designer clothes. The least popular are often dressed in clothes that are two, three, or more fashion cycles out of date." Edward Jones, "The Clothes Make the Kid," American View magazine.
- Status is often determined by how you dress, not who you are.
  - A shirt that has an alligator or polo pony isn't just a shirt—it's a status symbol
  - "A student who wears 'retro' clothing will often be seen as 'cool' or 'hip,' while someone who wears polyester trousers and a pocket protector will be stereotyped as a 'nerd' or 'dork'—even though he may be just as 'hip' as she." Jamie Ernstein, professor of Cultural Studies, personal interview.
- Logos and labels have now become part of the design in clothing. A T-shirt that used to have a picture or geometric design will now sport the company's logo.
- If everyone has to wear uniforms, the social divisions created by those who can afford designer clothing and those who can't will disappear.
- Students will be judged for who they are, not for what they wear.

► Lesson 11

Practice 1

Here are two sample profiles and sentences that establish each source's credibility.

"Fact" 1:	The average television channel shows 579 acts of violence in a 24-hour period.
Source:	Emily Rhodes
Profile:	Professor of Communications, New Jersey State University Founder, American Society for Media Responsibility Author of four books on the relationship between television and violence
Sentence:	According to Emily Rhodes, Professor of Communications at New Jersey State University and author of four books on the relationship between television and violence, the average television channel shows 579 acts of violence in a 24-hour period.

"Fact" 2:	Violent crimes committed by juveniles have quadrupled since 1973.
Source:	Children's Watch
Profile:	Nonprofit organization
	Studies children's issues, including crime, child labor, abuse, etc.
	Affiliated with New York State University
	Their annual report, "The State of Our Children," is required reading for the UN, WHO, and governmental policymakers
Sentence:	Children's Watch, a nonprofit dedicated to researching children's issues, claims that the number of violent crimes committed by juveniles has quadrupled since 1973—a fact that won't be overlooked by the government, since the group's annual report, "The State of Our Children," is required reading for members of both the House of Representatives and the Senate.

Practice 2

Answers will vary, but must contain all four elements.

1. Thesis: Despite the dangers, the Internet should remain a totally free and uncensored medium.
2. Supporting Points:
   - Censorship would violate the right to free speech.
   - Censorship of material on the Internet could set a precedent for censorship of other media.
   - The courts would be clogged with cases regarding censorship because the definition of whatever material should be censored would necessarily be vague and subject to interpretation.
3. The Opposition's Position:
   - Hate speech, when it incites violence, does not fall under protection of the First Amendment.
   - Nudity, cursing, and violence are limited on television, which kids can access 24 hours a day. How is the Internet different? Kids can access it 24 hours a day, too, with potentially no one around to control which sites they visit.
   - Determining what kind of material should be censored will lead to a nationwide examination of our values.
4. Paragraph Acknowledging the Opposition:
   Most importantly, censorship on the Internet violates one of the principles upon which this country was founded: freedom of speech. It is true that some sites present lewd or hateful images and ideas, but this kind of hate speech can be found anywhere, in all kinds of publications and all kinds of media. The Internet just makes it easier for people to find this information. If someone really wants to commit an act of violence, a website isn't what going to push him or her into committing a hate crime.

▶ Lesson 12

Practice 1

This example uses surprising facts to catch the reader's attention:

At Jamestown Senior High, an amazing thing happened. In just one year, student thefts dropped from 58 to 18, assaults plunged from 32 to 5, and total disciplinary action plummeted from 112 to 42. The dramatic change at Jamestown High was created by the institution of a simple policy, one that should be instituted at middle and high schools nationwide: school uniforms.

Practice 2

In this introduction, an anecdote is used:

Paula always wore the same two or three outfits. She decided she'd rather be made fun of for wearing the same clothes all the time than for wearing the cheap, no-name gear that made up most of her wardrobe. At least these outfits gave her a shot at hanging out with the cool kids. At least she could proudly display the brand-name logos.

Unfortunately, Paula's attitude toward clothing is all too common among students who spend more time worrying about what they (and others) are wearing than about what they're supposed to be learning. School uniforms can help change that—and help fix a number of other problems that are plaguing our schools.

► Lesson 13

Practice 1 and 2

Following are two possible conclusions for the school uniforms essay.
Closing with a question:

Of course, school uniforms won't solve every problem. Low-income kids will still be poor, violent students may still be violent, and advertisements will still assail us with the message that you can get what you want (the right guy, the right girl, the right friends, the right job) by buying and wearing trendy clothes. But school uniforms can help equalize the incredible division between the fashion "haves" and the "have nots"; they can improve discipline, and they can improve learning. In the same year the disciplinary incidents went down at Jamestown High, SAT scores went up. Wouldn't you like your school to do the same?

Closing with a call to action:

School uniforms aren't a cure-all, but in all of the public schools where school uniforms are now required, attendance and test scores are up, and disciplinary incidents are down. Students attest to feeling as if they're part of a community, and most say they like not having to worry about what to wear. More importantly, most say they actually feel better about themselves and school than they ever did before.

The power to create this kind of positive change is in your hands. Talk to your PTA and school board representatives. Show them the facts. Start a campaign to make school uniforms part of your child's education. You'll be glad you did—and so will they.

▶ Lesson 14

Practice 1

Following is an additional supporting paragraph. Notice how its first sentence uses the word *example*.

Here's another example. Imagine you're at a diner. When the server hands you your check, you notice that she made a mistake, charging you $12.58 instead of $15.58. But you don't tell her. Instead, you pay $12.58 and pocket the $3.00 difference.

Practice 2

This example revises and expands one of the paragraphs in the *lying with silence* essay:
Original:

I'm guilty, too. I knew my friend's boyfriend was also seeing someone else. But I kept quiet. I helped keep her in the dark. Then, when she found him out—and found out that I'd known about it—it was terrible. It destroyed their relationship and our friendship.

Revised and expanded:

I'm guilty of silent deceptions, too. For example, last year, I discovered that my friend Amy's boyfriend, Scott, was also seeing someone else. But I kept quiet about it because I didn't want to hurt Amy. A few weeks later, some-one else told her about Scott's two-timing—and told her that I knew about it.

Amy couldn't believe I deceived her like that. She felt just as betrayed as if I'd lied to her face about it. Scott's deception ruined their relationship. My deception ruined our friendship.

▶ Lesson 15

Practice 1

Your table should look something like this:

PARAGRAPH	IDEA	FUNCTION
3	when silence is a lie	addressing possible counterargument (that being silent isn't lying)
4	man who buys a necklace he knows is stolen	offers example of lie
5	consequences of his lie	offers evidence that silent lie is devastating
6	lying to Amy about Scott and consequences of that lie	offers another example and evidence of consequences
7	lying at diner	offers another example of silent lie
8	silent lies can be devastating; prosecute people who tell silent lies, not just "regular" lies	concludes essay

1. The essay is organized by order of importance, from most important to least important.
2. Probably not. For arguments, the best strategy is typically least to most important.
3. Reverse the order of the examples. Start with the diner scenario. Keep the Amy/Scott example second, and then end with the most powerful example—the man who knowingly bought a stolen necklace and gave it to his girlfriend.

Practice 2

Here's one way to revise the conclusion:

Silence can not only be deceitful—it can also be deadly. Before you decide to deceive someone with silence, consider the consequences of your action, and recognize it for what it is: a lie.

▶ Lesson 16

Practice 1

Individual revisions will vary, but you should have addressed the following problems in the paragraph.

1st sentence:	unnecessary repetition and wordiness
2nd sentence:	unnecessary repetition and wordiness, passive sentence
3rd sentence:	pretentious language and wordiness
4th sentence:	passive sentence
5th sentence:	unnecessary repetition and ambiguity (does *they* refer to questions or opportunities?)

Here's how the edited paragraph might look:

The greatest challenge my generation will face will be ethical dilemmas created by scientific advances. We have discovered so much in this century, especially in the last few decades. We have opportunities to do things we never thought possible before. But these opportunities have raised some very difficult ethical questions. These opportunities have given us new power over nature, but this power can easily be abused.

Practice 2

The following is an example of a successful edit.

My generation will face many problems. First is the problem of feeling overwhelmed by technology. Second, with the ever-increasing life span of human beings, the generation gap is widening. A third problem is the population explosion; there are more people on the planet than ever before, and the world population continues to grow exponentially, putting a squeeze on our habitable space. That leads us to a fourth problem: limited natural resources.

▶ Lesson 17

Practice 1

Here is the paragraph with run-ons, fragments, agreement errors, and confusing words corrected:

Comic relief is important in tragedies. Readers need a little relief from all of the sadness in the story. For example, consider Hamlet. After Ophelia dies, the next scene is with the gravedigger, who is a very funny character. He digs up a skull and makes a long speech about who the skull might have belonged to. Even though it is about death, the scene is funny, and it allows readers forget about the tragedy for a moment and laugh.

Practice 2

Here is the paragraph with capitalization, punctuation, and spelling errors corrected:

Compact discs (CDs), which may be found in over 25 million American homes, not to mention backpacks and automobiles, first entered popular culture in the 1980s. But their history goes back to the 1960s, when an inventor named James Russell decided to create an alternative to his scratched and warped phonograph records—a system that could record, store, and replay music without ever wearing out.

▶ Lesson 18

Practice 1

Each response will vary. Here's one that successful fulfills the assignment:

Thesis: One of today's unsung heroes is my friend Mani Kaur.
Outline:

1. How I met Mani
   * behind her in line at the store
   * she was buying diapers
   * couldn't believe how many she was buying
   * I asked if she needed help carrying them to her car
   * found out she had just adopted three baby girls from China

2. Meeting the babies
   * told Mani I loved children
   * she invited me to come over and help out
   * went the next day
   * saw how great she was with the babies.
   * saw how ill two of them looked

3. Why she adopted
   * told me about the law of having only one child
   * Mani and her husband couldn't have children of their own
   * wanted to rescue as many as they could, give them a better life

4. How can she handle it?
   * Mani's job—low paying (librarian), but flexible hours and close by
   * husband's job as marketing representative pays better, but he must travel three weeks each month
   * close network of family and friends to help out

5. Why is she a hero?
- forever changing lives of three children
- giving them a chance to grow up in a safe, loving home
- setting an example for others, like me
- a year later, babies all healthy, happy, well adjusted

Conclusion: Now when Mani goes to buy diapers, she always has someone to help—me.

▶ Lessons 19 and 20

Practice
To estimate a grade for your timed essay, look at the scoring chart on pages 174–175. Read your essay and evaluate it by using this special scoring system. After you assign a number for each of the categories shown on the scoring chart, average the numbers to get an overall score. A 5 is an "A," a 4 is a "B," and so on.

▶ Posttest, Part 1

If you miss any of the answers, you can find help for that question type in the lesson(s) shown to the right of the answer.

QUESTION	ANSWER	LESSON
1.	b.	1, 2
2.	d.	1
3.	c.	12
4.	a.	9
5.	d.	6, 7
6.	b.	10
7.	d.	9, 15
8.	a.	2
9.	c.	14–17
10.	b.	16
11.	a.	13
12.	a.	6, 7
13.	c.	17
14.	b.	18

QUESTION	ANSWER	LESSON
15.	b.	12
16.	d.	16
17.	e.	5, 8
18.	b.	5, 6
19.	d.	15
20.	a.	11

▶ Posttest, Part 2

Use the scoring chart on pages 174–175 to evaluate your essay. After you assign a number for each of the categories shown on the chart, average the numbers to get an overall score.

Additional Resources

▶ Grammar and Mechanics

Websites

www.grammarbook.com: the popular Blue Book of Grammar and Punctuation online, with simple explanations of grammar and punctuation pitfalls, and separate exercises and answer keys

www.m-w.com: Merriam-Webster Online. This site has a number of interesting features that will make you forget you are trying to improve your spelling! Check out the Word for the Wise section (www.m-w.com/cgi-bin/wftw.pl) for fun facts about words.

www.protrainco.com/info/grammar.htm: The Professional Training Company's "Good Grammar, Good Style Pages"

www.spelling.hemscott.net: Useful advice on how to improve your spelling

www.wsu.edu/~brians/errors/index.html: Paul Brians's "Common Errors in English"

Books

Castley, Anna, *Practical Spelling: The Bad Speller's Guide to Getting It Right Every Time* (LearningExpress, 1998)

Fowler, H.W., revised by Robert W. Burchfield, *The New Fowler's Modern English Usage*, 3rd Edition (Oxford University Press, 2005)

Johnson, Edward D., *The Handbook of Good English* (Washington Square Press, 1991)

LearningExpress, *1001 Vocabulary and Spelling Questions: Fast, Focused Practice to Help You Improve Your Word Skills* (LearningExpress, 1999)

LearningExpress, *Grammar Essentials, 3rd Edition* (LearningExpress, 2006)

Merriam-Webster, *Merriam-Webster's Guide to Punctuation and Style* (Merriam-Webster, 2002)

O'Conner, Patricia T., *Woe Is I: The Grammarphobe's Guide to Better English in Plain English*, 2nd Edition (Riverhead Trade, 2004)

Princeton Review, *Grammar Smart: A Guide to Perfect Usage*, 2nd Edition (Princeton Review, 2001)

Strunk, William, and E.B. White, *The Elements of Style*, 4th Edition (Longman, 2000)

Williams, Joseph M., *Style: Toward Clarity and Grace* (University of Chicago Press, 1995)

▶ Essay Exam Information

- **ACT**

  Online information, study tips, and practice test: www.actstudent.org.

  Books: The creator of the ACT published *The Real ACT Prep Guide* in 2004 (Peterson's Guides). Try Learning-Express's *ACT Exam Success in Only 6 Steps*.

- **SAT**

  Online information from the creator of the SAT: www.collegeboard.com.

  Books: Since the SAT essay was given for the first time in 2005, be certain you use only the latest editions of SAT preparation and information books. Good ones include *Acing the SAT*, published by LearningExpress, and *10 Real SATs*, published by The College Board.

- **GED**

  www.philaliteracy.org/tech/essay/ is the Mayor of Philadelphia's Commission on Literacy's site on how to prepare for the GED essay.

  Books: Check out LearningExpress's *Acing the GED*.

- **Regents'**

  www.gsu.edu/~wwwrtp/ is the state of Georgia Regents' Site, with sample essay test form, list of topics, and scoring information. Search for specific information on your state's test using your state name and "Regent's essay" as search terms.

▶ Supplemental Writing Prompts

501 Writing Prompt Questions (LearningExpress, 2003)

www.4tests.com has free practice tests modeled on the ACT, GED, and SAT essay sections, plus links to many good test-preparation sites.

▶ Online Writing Resources

www.bartleby.com

Without a doubt, the best online reference site on the Web. It has a searchable database of reference guides, encyclopedias, and much more. Just some of the works you'll find here include *The American Heritage Dictionary of the English Language, Fowler's Modern English Usage, The Elements of Style*, and *The American Heritage Book of English Usage*.

http://webster.commnet.edu/grammar/
This guide to grammar and writing, maintained by Professor Charles Darling of Capital Community College, Hartford, CT, is a comprehensive site with a particularly useful "ask grammar" service.

http://dir.yahoo.com/social_science/linguistics_and_human_languages/languages/specific_languages/english/grammar__usage__and_style/
Links to about 30 grammar and usage resources

http://www.askoxford.com
This site has sections on classic errors and helpful hints, better writing, and ask the experts. You can sign up for "word of the day" e-mails, or chat with others about language questions.

http://www.wsu.edu:8080/~brians/errors/index.html
Common Errors in English, by Paul Brians, Professor of English at Washington State University, is a thorough and easy-to-use site. William, James Co. has published a book based on this site titled *Common Errors in English Usage.*

▶ Suggestions for Great Writing

- *Harper's* (weekly magazine)
- *The Atlantic* (monthly magazine)
- *The Economist* (London-based weekly magazine; check it out online at www.economist.com)
- *The New Yorker* (weekly magazine)
- *Best American Essays 2005*, Susan Orlean, editor (Houghton Mifflin, 2005)
- *One Hundred Great Essays*, Robert DiYanni (Longman, 2001)
- *The Best American Science Writing 2005*, Alan Lightman, Jesse Cohen, editors (Harper Perennial, 2005)

NOTES

NOTES

NOTES

NOTES

NOTES

NOTES

Special FREE Online Practice from LearningExpress!

Let LearningExpress help you acquire essential writing skills FAST

Go to the LearningExpress Practice Center at www.LearningExpressFreeOffer.com, an interactive online resource exclusively for LearningExpress customers.

Now that you've purchased LearningExpress's *Write Better Essays in Just 20 Minutes a Day*, you have **FREE** access to:

- **A FREE online essay** to practice your narrative essay writing—instantly scored
- Examples and detailed answer **explanations of sample essays at different levels**
- Benchmark your skills and focus your study with our **customized diagnostic report**

Follow the simple instructions on the scratch card in your copy of *Write Better Essays in Just 20 Minutes a Day*. Use your individualized access code found on the scratch card and go to www.LearningExpressFreeOffer.com to sign in. Start practicing your essay-writing skills online right away!

Once you've logged on, use the spaces below to write in your access code and newly created password for easy reference:

Access Code: _____   Password: _____